It Happened At Niagara

Revised and Enlarged Edition

Sherman Zavitz

The Lundy's Lane Historical Society
Niagara Falls, Ontario, Canada
2014

Publishing History:

It Happened At Niagara
Revised and Enlarged Edition
Published by:
The Lundy's Lane Historical Society
Niagara Falls, Ontario, Canada L2G 1S9

Original printing 2008
Revised and reprinted 2010
Revised and reprinted 2014

It Happened At Niagara - First Series
Originally published in 1996 by
The Lundy's Lane Historical Society
in cooperation with
The Kiwanis Club of Stamford, Niagara Falls, Ontario
Revised Edition Published in 2001 by
The Lundy's Lane Historical Society

It Happened At Niagara - Second Series
Published in 1999 by
The Lundy's Lane Historical Society
Reprinted in 2001

It Happened At Niagara - Third Series
Published in 2003 by
The Lundy's Lane Historical Society

Front Cover Illustration:
Niagara Falls, The Horseshoe, circa 1852
Print from painting by Hippolyte Sebron
Sherman Zavitz Collection

ISBN 978-0-9682159-8-2

Dedication

Dedicated to the memory of Isabel Roberts Walker, Donald Loker,
Peter McKenna and Mildred Bromhall in tribute to their outstanding service
on behalf of The Lundy's Lane Historical Society.

Also dedicated in memory of
Nancy (Argenbright) Zavitz (1939-2002)

Foreword

The Lundy's Lane Historical Society, based in Niagara Falls, Ontario, was founded in 1887, making it the second oldest continuously operating organization of its kind in the province. From the beginning, one of the society's aims has been to make the story of Niagara's fascinating past better known to both residents and visitors. To that end, the society has published a number of books over the years, including *It Happened at Niagara*.

This revised and enlarged edition is a compilation of *It Happened At Niagara*, First, Second and Third Series. (The publishing history of these earlier volumes can be found on the reverse of the title page.) The stories have been arranged in a roughly chronological order. In addition, a number of stories have been partially or completely rewritten and three stories have been added.

As one of the crossroads of the world for over 150 years, Niagara Falls has played host to millions of visitors, including many well-known individuals. It has also been the site of a variety of dramatic and unusual happenings. As a result, there are many stories to be told and the society hopes that you will find those included in this edition of *It Happened At Niagara* to be both interesting and enjoyable.

Acknowledgements

As always, a book like this can only come together with the help of a number of people. My thanks, therefore, to Andrew Porteus and his wonderful staff in the Information Services Department of the Niagara Falls, Ontario, Public Library; April Petrie of The Niagara Parks Commission (now retired); the staff at the Special Collections, James A. Gibson Library, Brock University, St. Catharines, Ontario and the late Donald Loker who was the Local History Specialist at the Niagara Falls, New York, Public Library.

Special thanks are also due George Yerich, Sr., George Bailey, Robert Foley and Michael Brown for their assistance. Both Gill Tucker and my son, Michael Zavitz, were of great help with their keyboarding skills. A particular thank you goes to Helen Arkwright of the Robinson Library, University of Newcastle, Newcastle upon Tyne, England, for providing and granting permission to use Hugh Pattinson's photographs of Niagara Falls.

The stories in this book originally appeared in The Niagara Falls, Ontario, *Review* as part of a local history column entitled "A Niagara Note" that I have written for that newspaper since 1993. I appreciate the *Review's* willingness to support this type of feature.

I also want to express my gratitude to The Lundy's Lane Historical Society for its support. In particular, John Burtniak, longtime Society president and (now retired) Special Collections Librarian and University Archivist at Brock University, has been very helpful. Other Society members who have been members of the Publications Committee over the years include Margaret Lamb, the late Jim Mitchinson, Jim Healey and the late Peter Mckenna. My thanks to them as well as Darlene Teeuwsen of Just Details Graphic Design Studio and Larry Brooks of Commercial Digital Print for guiding my way. And to my wonderful wife, Ann, thank you for being such a true helpmate and inspiring partner.

Sherman Zavitz
Niagara Falls, Ontario
August 2014

The Niagara Parks Commission

Throughout this book you will find a number of references to The Niagara Parks Commission (NPC).

Founded in 1885, The Commission is a self-funding agency of the Ontario government. When first established, NPC controlled 62.2 hectares (154 acres) of land adjacent to the Horseshoe Falls on the Canadian side of the Niagara River. Today this public park system totals 1,325 hectares (3,274 acres), including 56 kilometres (35 miles) of roadway, stretching along the river from Fort Erie in the south to Niagara-on-the-Lake in the north.

NPC's mission is "To preserve and enhance the natural beauty of the Falls and the Niagara River corridor for the enjoyment of visitors while maintaining financial independence." The Commission generates income from restaurants, gift shops, parking lots, golf courses and various attractions.

Contents

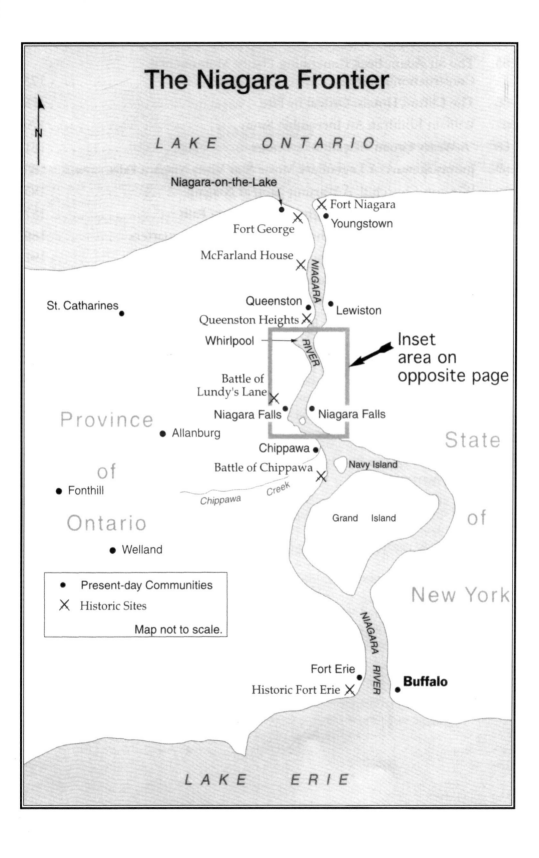

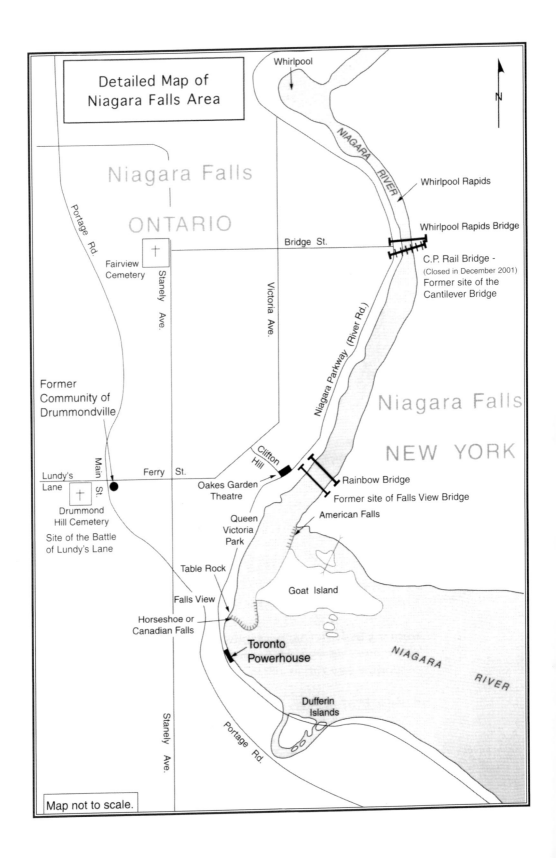

Detailed Map of
Niagara Falls Area

Whirlpool

N

Niagara Falls

ONTARIO

Portage Rd.

NIAGARA RIVER

Whirlpool Rapids

Bridge St.

Whirlpool Rapids Bridge

Fairview
Cemetery

Stanely Ave.

Victoria Ave.

Niagara Parkway (River Rd.)

C.P. Rail Bridge -
(Closed in December 2001)
Former site of the
Cantilever Bridge

Former
Community of
Drummondville

Niagara Falls

NEW YORK

Lundy's
Lane

Main St.

Ferry St.

Clifton
Hill

Rainbow Bridge

Oakes Garden
Theatre

Former site of Falls View Bridge

Drummond
Hill Cemetery

Queen
Victoria
Park

American Falls

Site of the Battle
of Lundy's Lane

Table Rock

Goat Island

Falls View

Horseshoe or
Canadian Falls

Toronto
Powerhouse

NIAGARA RIVER

Stanely Ave.

Portage Rd.

Dufferin
Islands

Map not to scale.

Organized A.D. 1887

Father Louis Hennepin:
The First European to See Niagara Falls

This depiction of Niagara Falls, the first ever made of the cataracts, appeared in Father Louis Hennepin's book *A New Discovery of a Vast Country in America* first published in 1697.

Betwixt the Lake Ontario and Lake Erie there is a vast and prodigious Cadence of Water which falls down after a surprising and astonishing manner, insomuch that the Universe does not afford its Parallel.

These words formed part of the first written description of Niagara Falls. They were penned by Father Louis Hennepin who, on December 7, 1678, became the first European to see this spectacle of nature.

It is interesting to visualize him standing in the snow at the edge of the gorge, clad in a coarse, gray, hooded cloak with the cord of St. Francis tied around his waist and a rosary and crucifix hanging at his side. Before him is the overwhelming blend of sight, sound and power that is Niagara, while at his back is the ancient forest, dense, cold and silent.

Louis Hennepin was born in Ath, Belgium, in 1626, and was trained for the priesthood in France. After travels in Italy, Germany and Holland, he was posted for a time in various convents in the towns of Calais and Dunkirk along the northern coast of France.

It was here that his romantic imagination was fired by the stories he heard from the sailors in these ports. He later wrote, "I hid myself behind tavern doors while the sailors were telling of their voyages. The tobacco smoke made me very sick at the stomach, but not withstanding, I listened attentively to all they said about their adventures at sea and their travels in distant countries. I could have passed whole days and nights in this way without eating."

His opportunity to have these kinds of experiences came in 1675, when he was ordered to sail for New France (Quebec) with the great explorer La Salle. After spending some time at the settlement of Quebec (now Quebec City), Hennepin was posted to Fort Frontenac (modern-day Kingston, Ontario) where La Salle was governor. It was from here that Hennepin sailed on November 18,

1678, as the missionary with a small expedition led by Sieur de la Motte, one of La Salle's associates.

Its destination was the Niagara River. Because of information supplied by Native North Americans, many of the early explorers in what is now Canada, including La Salle, were aware of Niagara Falls and knew their location but they had not actually seen the cataracts.

La Monte had orders to establish a warehouse below the Falls, and to find a location above the cataracts suitable for the construction of a ship that La Salle wanted to have for trade on the upper Great Lakes.

The mouth of the river was reached on December 6. On the following day Hennepin and several others set out on their own, travelling by canoe to as far as what is now Queenston. After landing there, they climbed the high ridge of land now known as the Niagara Escarpment and struggled through the wintry forest as the roar ahead of them grew louder and louder. Finally, after pushing back a mass of snow-laden tree boughs, the full majesty of Niagara Falls burst upon them. Hennepin was awed and wrote: "The waters which fall from this vast height do foam and boil after the most hideous manner imaginable, making an outrageous noise more terrible than that of thunder."

After moving on a short distance, the little party of men made camp that night along the banks of the Chippawa Creek. Hennepin mentions that the snow was about a foot deep and they had to dig it up before making their fire.

Over the next three years Hennepin did a considerable amount of travelling and exploration under the direction of La Salle. Much of this was on the Illinois and Mississippi Rivers. He also made several return visits to Niagara.

On April 12, 1680, as he and two companions were repairing their canoes along the banks of the Illinois, they were suddenly surrounded by a war party of Sioux. The men were carried off as prisoners to Sioux territory. Treated well, Hennepin made copious notes about the way of life he saw around him. On several occasions during that summer they were taken on hunting expeditions in what are now the states of Minnesota and Wisconsin.

Released that September, the men eventually made their way back to Niagara and then to Fort Frontenac and Montreal. Hennepin sailed from Quebec for Europe in the autumn of 1681.

Back home, he prepared an account of his travels and experiences. Published first in French in 1697, an English edition became available the following year. Entitled *A New Discovery of a Vast Country in America*, it became a best-seller and gave Europeans their first knowledge of Niagara Falls.

Only scattered bits of information exist concerning Hennepin's later years. He died about 1705.

Standing in Queen Victoria Park today is a blue and gold provincial plaque that honours Father Louis Hennepin as the first European to see Niagara Falls. It has been placed opposite the area of the gorge where the crest of the Falls would have been at the time of his discovery.

La Rochefoucault-Liancourt:
An Early Tourist

La Rochefoucault-Laincourt visited Niagara in June 1795.

From *LaRochefoucault-Liancourt's Travels in Canada 1795*. Edited with notes by William Renwick Riddell (1917).

Among Niagara's very early "tourists" was a member of the French aristocracy. Francois Alexandre Frederic La Rochefoucault-Liancourt, born in 1747, became a friend and advisor to both Kings Louis XV and XVI. In 1792 he was forced to take refuge in England, however, when the increasingly powerful revolutionary forces in France began to take exception to his close association with royalty.

During the winter of 1794-95 he decided to pay a visit to North America, and so crossed the Atlantic for, as he noted in his journal, "a journey for philosophical and commercial observation."

By June 1795 he had reached the Niagara frontier, and on the 21st of that month was rowed downriver from Fort Erie to Chippawa. La Rochefoucault was clearly full of anticipation at this point. He observed, "We were now approaching the prospect of the Grand Cataract of Niagara, one of the principal objects of our journey, and which I had long desired to see.... At last we heard the noise, and perceived the spray."

After landing at Chippawa, he and a companion mounted horses and rode to the Falls. He was awed at "the magnificent spectacle" and wrote, "It is impossible to describe the impression, which this cataract made upon our minds."

Almost immediately he felt compelled to climb down to the base of the Falls. It was a very perilous journey. Using a few steps cut into trees, hanging onto bushes and rocks, often crawling on his hand and knees, while realizing all the while that one false step could mean the end, he finally reached the river's edge. He was very pleased with himself at having successfully met such a challenge, and felt that it had been worth the effort.

Later that evening La Rochefoucault had dinner at Fort Chippawa, which was located on the site of what is now King's Bridge Park, about 1.6 kilometres (1 mile) above the Falls. His hosts were Captain James Hamilton and "his sweet and lovely wife, Louisa."

He describes the village of Chippawa as consisting of a "tolerable inn and a small number of other houses." An interesting observation in his journal is that the Chippawa Creek (Welland River) had very stagnant water which frequently resulted in fevers among the population. He also mentions that an iron mine had been recently discovered along the creek and a company was being formed to work it. (The substance was probably limonite, a mineral frequently found in marshy areas.)

The following morning he left Chippawa, in pouring rain, to once again see the Falls. This time he was taken to Table Rock. At that time this was a large shelf of rock that projected from the gorge wall, fairly close to the Horseshoe Falls. He was quite impressed with the location and noted, "It is from this spot that this wonder of nature should be viewed."

He found it curious, however, that the British government had not provided some cleared areas to make it easier to see the Falls. Apparently, the government's position was since so few people came to see Niagara it wasn't worth the expense to provide more convenient access.

La Rochefoucault had many more sights to see during his tour, but felt, "Nothing can stand the test of comparison with the Falls of Niagara."

Elizabeth Simcoe:
An Early Admirer of Niagara

Mrs. Elizabeth Simcoe was a frequent visitor to Niagara Falls and enjoyed staying at the home of Mrs. Gilbert Tice, which was located on the northwest corner of Mountain Road and Portage Road in present-day Niagara Falls. Elizabeth's tent can be seen at the right.

From *The Diary of Mrs. John Graves Simcoe*. With notes and a biography by J. Ross Robertson (1934).

"The fall itself is the grandest sight imaginable.... The prodigious spray which arises from the foam at the bottom of the fall adds grandeur to the scene which is wonderfully fine." These were some of the impressions written by Elizabeth Simcoe after she had viewed Niagara Falls for the first time. The date was Monday, July 30, 1792.

Elizabeth's husband, John Graves Simcoe, had been appointed the first Lieutenant-Governor of the new province of Upper Canada (Ontario). The couple had sailed from England on September 26, 1791 with two of their six children, Francis and Sophia. After spending the winter in Quebec City, they proceeded to Montreal, Kingston and York (Toronto). In the early morning of July 26, 1792, they sailed across Lake Ontario to Niagara (Niagara-on-the-Lake), which had been selected as the province's temporary capital. (Simcoe soon changed the name of the settlement to Newark.) Four days later Elizabeth and her husband made their first visit to the Falls of Niagara.

Mrs. Simcoe prided herself on being a keen observer. She was also a great diary and letter writer. Much of what she saw and did while in the Niagara area over the next four years was committed to paper and can still be read today. She also loved to sketch and paint. Fortunately, much of her Niagara art also survives, giving us a fascinating look at this area as it was over two centuries ago.

In her diary, Elizabeth goes on to mention that during that first visit to Niagara Falls they had refreshments on Table Rock. She was told that many ladies in particular did not like to go there because the area was infested with rattlesnakes.

They then travelled on above the Falls as far as Fort Chippawa, located about 1.6 kilometres (1 mile) above the cataracts. It was an exciting day for Elizabeth, marred only by a bad reaction to a mosquito bite that caused her arm to swell so badly that her sleeve had to be cut open.

Mrs. Simcoe was also very impressed with the whirlpool, a place she visited many times and described as "a very grand scene." After one such visit on April 24, 1793, she describes in her diary how, while riding back to Newark at dusk along the Niagara River, she observed that the Indians had set many fires along the riverside to attract the fish, which would then be speared.

On August 24, 1795, Governor Simcoe and Elizabeth, for the first time, climbed down into the Niagara Gorge opposite the American Falls. She was enthralled by the view from the water's edge and sat on a rock sketching the scene until her paper became damp with spray. She wrote that later in the day, before climbing back up the gorge, they "dined on the rocks beneath the overhanging cedars."

For several years, because of what she considered oppressive summer heat at Newark, Elizabeth spent some time at the home of Mrs. Gilbert Tice, located on the northwest corner of today's Portage and Mountain Roads in Niagara Falls. Here on the "Mountain" (Niagara Escarpment), she felt the air was fresher and healthier. She and her young son, Francis, frequently took riding or walking excursions from Mrs. Tice's to the Niagara River, so that their time "was filled up with seeing the most delightful scenery."

On August 14, 1795, she recorded this entry in her diary: "We pitched the tent near the Falls and dined, after which, being fatigued by the heat, I lay down in the tent and slept, lulled by the sound of the Falls which was going to sleep in the pleasantest way imaginable."

The Simcoes went back to England in 1796 and never returned to Canada. Elizabeth continued, however, to have a great interest in Canadian affairs until her death in 1850 at the age of 87. (Her husband had died in 1806.)

Elizabeth Simcoe was a passionate admirer of Niagara. Through her legacy of paintings, letters and her diary, we are able to go back over 200 years and see this area as she saw it, and appreciate her feelings of wonder, excitement and discovery.

Theodosia and Joseph Alston: The First Nuptial Tour to Niagara

Theodosia Burr Alston in 1802. She and her husband, Joseph, came to Niagara Falls as part of their nuptial tour in 1801.

Engraving from a painting by John Vanderlyn. In James Parton, *The Life and Times of Aaron Burr* (1858).

No place in the world is more famous as a honeymoon destination than Niagara Falls. The first recorded newlyweds arrived at Niagara in 1801, but an event that led up to that visit began four years earlier and involved the Indian chief, Joseph Brant (Thayendanegea).

This famous Mohawk was born in what is now northeast Ohio. He received a good education and for a number of years worked for the British Indian Department. In 1776 he visited England and was presented to King George III. During the American Revolution, he fought bravely for the Royal cause. In 1784, following the war, Brant led the Mohawks and other Six Nations people to new homes on a large tract of land on both sides of the Grand River in southern Ontario. Great Britain awarded them this land in gratitude for their loyal support during the American War of Independence and in compensation for the loss of Mohawk territory in New York State.

Brant remained an influential figure with both British and American governments. In 1797, President George Washington invited him to Philadelphia where he was received by many in society. One of these was Senator Aaron Burr, who was so delighted with Brant that he gave a private dinner in his honour.

The Senator, recently widowed, felt that his daughter, 14-year old Theodosia, should also meet the celebrated Mohawk. Accordingly, he made arrangements for Brant to visit her at Richmond Hill, Burr's palatial home in what is now the Greenwich Village section of New York City.

Theodosia was thrilled at meeting the illustrious Brant, and he was impressed by her charm, hospitality and intellect. She spoke, wrote and read five languages besides English, and could hold her own on any subject in conversation with the most renowned individuals. She could also skate, swim, ride and dance better, many said, than any other young lady in the country. Before leaving New York, Brant gave her an invitation to visit him in Canada.

In February 1801 Theodosia married Joseph Alston, who came from a wealthy Charleston, South Carolina family. The wedding, a magnificent affair, was held at Richmond Hill shortly after Aaron Burr had been elected Vice President of the United States.

The following July, the newlyweds set out on a delayed bridal tour (or nuptial tour) to the north during which Theodosia intended to include a visit with Joseph Brant. She also wanted to see Niagara Falls, something her father had encouraged her to do. Nine pack horses and many servants accompanied the couple during the long and difficult journey through the wilderness of New York State.

After reaching the little village of Buffalo, the Alstons went on to see the great Falls

Theodosia Alston was able to meet Joseph Brant, the distinguished Mohawk Indian Chief.

From *Memoir of Capt. Joseph Brant* (1872).

of Niagara, arriving here in late July. That Theodosia was impressed with the cataracts is evident by what she wrote in a letter to her sister-in-law, "If you wish to have an idea of real sublimity, visit the Falls of Niagara – they are magnificent; words when applied to express their grandeur appear to lose half their significance – to describe them is impossible; they must be seen."

After viewing the Falls, the couple travelled downriver to Queenston where they stayed at an inn operated by Joshua Fairbanks. They then journeyed westward for their rendezvous with Joseph Brant, which took place either at his lovely Georgian manor house at Burlington Bay or his home along the Grand River near present-day Brantford. Theodosia and Joseph continued their "northern journey," as they styled it, by moving on to York (Toronto), Kingston, Montreal and Quebec City before turning south. The tour was a great success.

In the years that followed, however, fate was not kind to the Alstons. In May 1802, Theodosia gave birth to a son christened Aaron Burr Alston. Never did a child have more adoring parents or a prouder grandfather.

Tragically, however, the little boy died of malarial fever on June 30, 1812. Devastated, Theodosia wrote to her father: "There is no more joy for me. The world is a blank. I have lost my boy."

Six months later, on December 30, 1812, Joseph, who had just been elected governor of South Carolina, saw his wife off as she boarded a chartered vessel that was to take her from Georgetown, South Carolina, to New York to see her father. The ship was lost at sea and no trace of it or Theodosia was ever found. These personal tragedies weighted heavily on Joseph and seemed to hasten his death, which came on September 10, 1816. He was only 38.

Joseph and Theodosia are often referred to as Niagara Falls' first honeymooners. In a sense, this is true. However, as we have seen, the Alstons were actually on what was called a bridal or nuptial tour. Common in the early 1800s, these trips often included family members and, if one were wealthy enough, even servants. The tour, sometimes taken months after the marriage, was for the purpose of visiting relatives and friends who had not been at the wedding.

Theodosia and Joseph were the first recorded couple to visit Niagara Falls on a bridal tour. They were well-known trendsetters. As a result, other newly-married couples also started coming to Niagara Falls as part of their bridal tour. By the 1830s the nuptial/bridal trip was beginning to evolve into the wedding trip or honeymoon, with couples taking a private, romantic trip to Niagara Falls immediately after their wedding. A famous, enduring tradition had been firmly established.

T.C.:
A Ride to Niagara in 1809

This engraving, originally published in 1804, was taken from a painting by the celebrated American artist, John Vanderlyn. Seen from the Canadian side, both the American and Canadian (Horseshoe) Falls are clearly visible. T.C., arriving in 1809, would have viewed a virtually identical scene.

From Charles Mason Dow, *Anthology and Bibliography of Niagara Falls* (1921).

On Saturday, May 6, 1809, a traveller, who in his journal identifies himself only as T.C. (a.k.a. Thomas Cooper), set out on horseback from the central Pennsylvania town of Williamsport to visit Niagara Falls.

This was by no means an easy journey to undertake. While travel today often requires some stamina and patience, it must have taken unbelievable amounts of each in 1809. A sense of humour would have helped as well. T.C. stayed at inns that he describes as "bad," or "miserable," sometimes "tolerable," and only rarely "good." The roads were occasionally "pleasant," often "very bad," and sometimes downright "villainous."

T.C. persevered, however, and eight days later reached Buffalo. Here he crossed the Niagara River by ferry and proceeded along "an excellent road through good land" to Chippawa. He described that community as having about ten houses along with two taverns or inns. He stayed at the one kept by a man named Stevens, describing it as a good tavern with a large, carpeted dining room.

When our traveller attempted to get directions about reaching and viewing the Falls, however, he found his host not particularly helpful. All Stevens could tell him was, "They are by the riverside, you cannot miss them."

Armed with this rather vague information, T.C. set out from Chippawa on May 15 to find the Falls of Niagara. He first went along Portage Road to a spot just north of where the building that formerly housed Loretto Christian Life Centre is now. From here he followed what was called the Wagon or Mill Road that went down the side of the embankment ending at a spot about 800 metres (half a mile) above the Horseshoe Falls.

In the early 1800s, this area, roughly between the present-day Niagara Parks Floral Showhouse and the Canadian Niagara Power Plant, was known as "The Flats." The Niagara River ran closer to the base of the high bank. Using this water for power, a number of industries had developed in the area. T.C. wrote, for example, that he noticed some mills and a tannery. (At one point, a distillery operated in the vicinity of where the Floral Showhouse is now located.)

At one of these industries, he found someone to escort him to the Falls. He was taken to Table Rock, which at that time was still a large shelf of rock projecting from the gorge wall, fairly close to the Horseshoe Falls. It was only a short distance, but he described the walk as "uncomfortable" because the path was very winding and there was so much undergrowth to get through.

T.C. found the scene from Table Rock one of "grandeur and beauty, unrivaled. I felt content that I had taken the journey. It was worth the trouble."

He was critical, however, of the Chippawa innkeepers. Considering the fact that some of their business came from visitors wanting to see the Falls of Niagara, he felt that they could not only be more helpful, but also improve the pathways and viewing areas around the Falls. As it was, he considered that it must be particularly "arduous and fatiguing for the female sex."

Our traveller went on to the whirlpool and then visited Queenston. A highlight there was "a pint of excellent port" which he found to be "the fashionable wine among the Anglo Canadians."

Back home in Pennsylvania, T.C. worked the notes that he had made during his trip into something of a guide (complete with a map) for others "who have the leisure and curiosity to visit an object so remarkable as Niagara Falls."

John De Cew:
A Daring Escape and a Remarkable Walk | 6

Like many pioneers in the Niagara area, John De Cew faced a number of experiences that tested his skill, courage and resourcefulness. One particular episode of this type, however, was to stand out above all others.

De Cew had been born in Vermont in 1766. He came to Canada as an United Empire Loyalist in the late 1780s, and soon obtained a large tract of

The house (now destroyed) of John DeCew, near DeCew Falls, circa 1900.

From *Pen Pictures of Early Pioneer Life in Upper Canada* (1905).

land located on the west branch of the Twelve Mile Creek along the brow of the Niagara Escarpment, just south of where the Brock University campus in St. Catharines is now located.

He built a number of mills at the site and threw himself into the work of a pioneer industrialist, as well as managing a large farm. The area became known as De Cew Falls.

After his marriage in 1798, De Cew built a large, two-storey stone house which became the marvel of the area at the time and was to play a part in Canadian history. It was at this house, during the War of 1812, that Laura Secord ended her now-famous 32-kilometre (20-mile) walk from Queenston on June 22, 1813. She had overheard information that the Americans were planning to attack Lieutenant James Fitzgibbon and his troops who were headquartered at De Cew's home. Demonstrating considerable courage, she undertook the exhausting, day-long walk to warn Fitzgibbon. (This historic stone house was destroyed by fire in 1950. The foundation has been preserved as an historic site.)

John De Cew was not at home to see Laura Secord. In fact, the greatest trial of his life had begun just a few days before. While on duty as a captain in the Lincoln Militia, he was captured by an American raiding party. A number of other men were also taken the same way. On the very day of Laura's walk they were all transported across the Niagara River and imprisoned at Fort Niagara. There followed a number of moves, with De Cew and 16 others finally being sent to the Invincible Prison in Philadelphia.

While there the men decided to try and make an escape. On the wall at the one end of their common room was a large fireplace which backed onto a street.

The chimney was large enough for a man to get through but was blocked by a grate of iron bars. Each day, during the time they were usually left alone, the prisoners began cutting through the bars using the mainsprings of their watches for saws. One of the men played on his fife to drown out the noise of the sawing. Just before the chimney underwent its daily inspection, they wrapped the grate with paper that had been rubbed in soot.

Finally, a large enough hole had been made and the escape was set for eight o'clock on the evening of April 20, 1814. It was raining that night as each man carefully climbed up through the chimney and let himself down the outside by using a rope of bedding sheets that had been tied together. When John, the last to escape, had reached the top of the chimney and was ready to make his descent, he found, to his horror, that the man who had preceded him had broken the rope. He had no choice but to drop to the ground. Injuring his foot in the fall, he told the others to leave him and make good their escape.

Later, De Cew hobbled into the wet, dark and deserted streets. Realizing he had to have help, he noticed a house with a lighted candle in the window and, after gaining admittance, threw himself on the mercy of the owners. He was very lucky. They agreed to hide him in a hayloft over a stable.

The next day the Quaker owner of the house showed him a handbill offering a reward of one hundred dollars for the capture of each one of the escaped prisoners, and announcing that anyone found concealing a prisoner or helping in their escape would be charged with high treason. Considering the great danger, De Cew told his host to turn him in and collect the reward. The Quaker told him, however, that his conscience would never allow him to do that.

After three days, John was given new clothes and some money to help him get back to Canada. Deciding that he should not attempt to go by way of the Niagara River, he chose a route through New York State and Vermont to the Quebec border. Keeping to back trails, swamps and woods to avoid detection by enemy troops, De Cew walked some 644 kilometres (400 miles), all of it in constant pain from the broken bone in his foot.

Successfully crossing into Canada, he soon found himself, as he later wrote, "in a British camp surrounded by redcoats and my beloved Union Jack." He was given a pass to get back to his Niagara home, thus completing a truly remarkable journey. Rejoining his regiment, De Cew was present at the Battle of Lundy's Lane which took place in what is now Niagara Falls, Ontario, on July 25, 1814. He did not take part in the fighting, but was placed in charge of the commissariat.

Although his foot never properly healed and bothered him for the rest of his life, De Cew suffered no other ill effects from his wartime experience. He was 89 years old when he died in 1855.

"By The Bayonet": The Taking of Fort Niagara

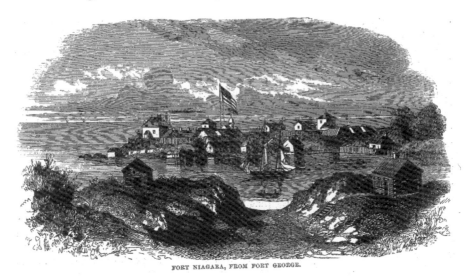

FORT NIAGARA, FROM FORT GEORGE.

A view of Fort Niagara, looking across the Niagara River from Fort George, as it looked in the time of the War of 1812.

From Benson J. Lossing, *The Pictorial Field-Book of the War of 1812* (1868).

It is 1 a.m., December 19, 1813.

In the darkness and freezing cold, a force of 562 British and Canadian soldiers is assembled along the bank of the lower Niagara River, just north of what is known today as the McFarland House. In a few minutes, using boats with muffled oars, the men are carried across to the American side, landing at a point about 4 kilometres (2.5 miles) above Fort Niagara.

This stronghold at the mouth of the river is their goal, but absolute silence is essential since it is to be a surprise attack. As they disembark, every soldier knows exactly why this mission is being undertaken – revenge.

The War of 1812 was in its second year. On May 27, 1813, the Americans had captured Fort George. They held it, along with the nearby town of Niagara (now Niagara-on-the-Lake) and the outlying area until the following December. On the 10th of that month, American commander George McClure decided to abandon Fort George and retreat across the Niagara River. Before doing so, however, he ordered his soldiers to put the torch to Niagara.

Most of the town's men were with the militia or in prison at Fort Niagara. The homes were occupied only by women, children and old, sick men. All were forced into the snowy streets with, in many cases, little more than the clothes on their backs. One woman, too ill to walk, was carried out in her bed and left lying in the snow to watch her home be destroyed. In all, about 130 buildings were burned that night, leaving 400 people homeless.

Lieutenant-General Gordon Drummond, commander in Upper Canada (Ontario) and Colonel John Murray soon decided on a retaliatory attack for this senseless destruction and suffering. The plan was to first take Fort Niagara and then, with help from Mohawk forces, sweep up the east side of the Niagara River all the way to Buffalo, destroying every community along the way.

Now Murray leads his troops through the snow on a frigid, moonless night. They have been told that all killing is to be silent. Drummond has ordered Fort Niagara to be taken "by the bayonet."

At the village of Youngstown, a shivering American sentry is spotted outside a tavern. Sergeant Andrew Spearmen creeps up to the guard, and while half-choking him, demands the password to Fort Niagara. After getting it, Spearmen kills him.

Murray then looks through the tavern window. Inside he sees 20 members of the American advance guard whose officers are playing a game of whist. The British Colonel and several aides stealthily move through the front door. At this point, one of the American officers, totally unaware of the enemy a few metres away in the shadows, asks, "What's trump?" Murray yells, "Bayonets!" He then leads the charge into the room. In a matter of a few minutes, all the Americans are dead. The British and Canadians then continue their silent march along the river.

At around five o'clock they reach the main gate of Fort Niagara. The draw-bridge is down while sentries are being changed. Sergeant Spearman walks across the bridge, is challenged, gives the password and mumbles something about Youngstown. As the sentry turns, Spearman bayonets him. The entire force then storms the gate and charges across the parade ground.

Fort Niagara is soon in British hands. Colonel Murray hauls down the American flag and replaces it with a Union Jack.

This story has a fascinating 20th century footnote involving that captured American flag. Murray presented it to Gordon Drummond who, in turn, sent the flag to King George III. Some years later, his successor, George IV, returned it to the Drummond family.

When it was learned that the flag still existed, the Old Fort Niagara Association purchased it for $150,000, and in March 1994, this rare piece of American history was returned to Fort Niagara, 181 years after it had left. It is a tangible reminder of a very dramatic night along the Niagara River many years ago.

Cecil Bisshopp: A Raid Goes Wrong

It is 2 a.m. July 11, 1813.

In the darkness and mist, some 200 British and Canadian soldiers embark from the Canadian side of the Niagara River, a short distance downstream from Fort Erie. Their objectives are the fortifications and stores at Black Rock on the American side of the river, near Buffalo.

The success of their operation is important since the troops are in desperate need of many supplies, from shoes (particularly for the 41st Regiment which has none) to salt, which the commissariat needs to preserve pork.

Lieutenant-Colonel Cecil Bisshopp was buried in what is now Drummond Hill Cemetery in 1813. The simple marker placed over his grave was destroyed the following year during the Battle of Lundy's Lane, which raged through the little cemetery and the surrounding area. In 1846, Bisshopp's two sisters erected this memorial.

Photo by Sherman Zavitz.

The war of 1812 had begun just a little over a year before. In May of 1813, American forces had captured Fort George at the mouth of the Niagara River. Most of the British troops withdrew to the head of Lake Ontario. The enemy attempted several offensive operations during June, but was beaten on both occasions. By July, the invaders were being held at Fort George in a defensive situation, while the British were beginning to take some action along the Upper Niagara River again.

In charge of the raid on Black Rock is Lieutenant-Colonel Cecil Bisshopp. A career soldier, at 30 he has already seen service in Russia, Spain and Holland. He arrived in Canada in September 1812, anxious "to fight the Yankees" as he wrote. Greatly liked and respected by his men, he is heir to a title and a considerable fortune.

As silently as cats, the men make their way across the Niagara River and pounce on Black Rock. As is hoped, the Americans are taken completely by surprise. Soon the naval yard, barracks, blockhouses and a schooner are all in flames.

Several warehouses are quickly emptied of artillery and stores. The British and Canadians, who up to this point have not lost a man, realize that a quick getaway is important before the Americans can bring in reinforcements. Bisshopp, however, decides to take a chance and orders that 123 barrels of salt be removed from a warehouse and rolled down to the boats at the water's edge. It is a fatal error of judgment. As the boats are still being loaded, the Americans burst from the nearby woods. Bisshopp orders a retreat, while he leads a small detachment to meet the enemy and cover the withdrawal. A bullet suddenly shatters his left thigh. As he is carried to the riverbank, he is struck in the right wrist and shortly after, while being rowed back across the river, he is hit a third time.

Altogether, 38 British and Canadians are killed or wounded. Bisshopp's wounds are not considered serious, but he sinks into a deep depression, feeling personally responsible for the loss of life during the retreat. He loses the will to live and dies peacefully a few days later.

On July 17, 1813, Bisshopp was laid to rest in what is now known as Drummond Hill Cemetery, in present-day Niagara Falls. (The cemetery had been established in 1799.) Rev. Robert Addison, from St. Mark's Church at Niagara (now Niagara-on-the-Lake), conducted the service. His fellow officers then erected a stone over the grave.

One year later, the Battle of Lundy's Lane raged over the little cemetery and the surrounding area. All the gravestones were badly damaged.

In 1846, Cecil Bisshopp's two sisters erected a new memorial in tribute to, as part of the lengthy inscription reads, "...an excellent man and beloved brother." It may still be seen today – a memorial to a young soldier from long ago who, in the words of a writer at the time, "will be remembered...with the most enduring regret."

Joseph Willcocks:
Traitor

Joseph Willcocks, one of early Ontario's more enigmatic public figures, helps put the torch to what is now Niagara-on-the-Lake in December 1813.

Illustration by George Balbar. Courtesy of Haunted Press.

December 1813 was unusually cold and snowy.

For the resident of Niagara (now Niagara-on-the-Lake), the severe weather that month was a small worry compared to other concerns – the War of 1812 was also raging.

Since the preceding May, when the Americans had captured nearby Fort George, their town and the surrounding area had been under enemy occupation.

Now, in the early days of December, came the news that the foe was about to abandon the fort and move across the river to Fort Niagara. The most disturbing part of this story, however, was the rumour that the Americans were first going to fire the town.

As darkness fell on the evening of December 10, the rumor became a tragic fact. A group of U.S. soldiers, under the command of Brigadier-General George McClure, took up torches and began to set fire to virtually every house and public building in the town.

It was a wanton act of destruction.

Captain William Hamilton Merritt and his Provincial Dragoons rode into the town shortly after the Americans had fled across the Niagara River. He later wrote, "Nothing but heaps of coals, and the streets full of furniture that the inhabitants were fortunate to get out of their houses, met the eye in all directions."

Only one house was still standing.

During the height of the destruction, many of the citizens of Niagara recognized a man helping McClure and his soldiers torch their town. He was Joseph Willcocks who had at one time lived among them and was even a member of the Legislative Assembly of Upper Canada (Ontario).

Willcock's career presents one of the more interesting and puzzling case studies in early Ontario history.

Born in Ireland, he emigrated to Canada in 1800, settling in York (now Toronto). Here, a relative of Willcocks soon helped him get a job as a clerk for Receiver-General Peter Russell. Things went very well for Willcocks and after only a few weeks, he was on such good terms with his employer that he was even given a room in Russell's house, becoming almost a member of the family. After a few months, however, events turned sour. Also living in the house was Russell's unmarried sister whom Willcocks began to court. When Peter Russell learned of this, he fired his clerk and threw him out of the house with, as Willcocks wrote in his diary, "much violent language."

He still had many influential and sympathetic friends, however, and before long, he was appointed sheriff of York. About this time, Willcocks began to be very close to those who openly opposed the government. Informers brought word to Governor Francis Gore that Willcocks had made some indiscreet remarks. He was immediately dismissed as sheriff.

Willcocks then went to New York, bought a printing press and type and, coming to Niagara in September 1807, set up a newspaper. Calling it the *Upper Canada Guardian* or *Freeman's Journal*, the paper openly attacked leading officials, denounced the government and spoke out on behalf of the isolated settlers.

Enough of them supported him to bring about his election to the Legislative Assembly in 1808, and again in 1812, as a member for Lincoln. (This riding took in most of the Niagara Peninsula.) There continued to be consequences, however, from some of his activities and statements. He even spent some time in jail for contempt of parliament.

Willcocks, and those he came to lead in opposition to the government, was against all measures that would place Upper Canada in a state of defence against any American attack. This alarmed Major-General Isaac Brock, who became the administrator and commander of the forces in Upper Canada in 1811. He invited Willcocks to dinner one evening shortly after the outbreak of war with the Americans in June 1812. Within a few hours, the former enemy of the government had made a complete turnabout. He pledged his support to Brock. During the Battle of Queenston Heights, October 13, 1812, Willcocks bravely fought for the British.

However, after the death of Brock at Queenston Heights, and with the Americans gaining some advantages in early 1813, Willcocks switched his loyalty and in July of that year went over to the American side. He gathered around him a number of other expatriate Upper Canadians and formed them into a mounted force, calling it The Canadian Volunteers. Supported by the American army, they conducted raids around the Niagara Peninsula and fought alongside the invaders.

By November 1813, Willcocks and his men had unleashed a reign of terror in the Niagara area, robbing settlers of household goods, burning homes and barns, and arresting people for no other reason than that they were loyal to the government.

He stooped to his lowest point, however, on that fateful night of December 10, 1813, when he led the Americans around Niagara, helping to put the town to the torch.

On September 4, 1814, Willcocks and his Volunteers were helping the Americans defend Fort Erie against a British assault. As he led a detachment against a British position, Joseph Willcocks, traitor, was shot dead.

To the residents of burned-out Niagara, the news of his death must have brought a grim satisfaction.

Upper Canada's (Ontario's) first opposition newspaper was the *Upper Canada Guardian* or *Freeman's Journal*. It was published by Joseph Willcocks at what is now Niagara-on-the-Lake. This issue is dated April 14, 1810.

From J.E. Middleton, *The Romance of Ontario* (1931).

John Le Couteur:
"Dead Bodies in all Directions"

A group of exhausted British soldiers rest among the dead and dying following the bloody Battle of Lundy's Lane, July 25, 1814. One of the soldiers was Lieutenant John Le Couteur.

Illustration by George Balbar. Courtesy of Haunted Press.

A bleak twilight envelops the snow-shrouded desolation of the New Brunswick wilderness. Making its way in silent misery through this forlorn scene is a long column of soldiers, their bodies numbed to the core. It is so cold they can scarcely breathe. The temperature is 27 degrees below zero.

It is March 5, 1813, and the 104th Regiment of Foot is on a march from Fredericton to Quebec City. Temporarily in charge is Lieutenant John Le Couteur. That night, as he continues to shiver even by the fire, Le Couteur writes in his journal: "The intensity of the cold is indescribable. When we got to the end of our day's march the cold was so intense that the men could scarcely use their fingers to hew down the firewood, or to build huts, and it was dark before we could commence cooking, if sticking a bit of salt pork on the end of a twig and holding it in a fire could be so termed."

Frostbite was common, one man becoming an ulcerated mass "as if scalded all over from boiling water." Those in charge of the supply toboggans frequently had to struggle with snowdrifts around three metres (10 feet) in depth.

Despite the cold and privations, the regiment reached Quebec City without the loss of a single man, only to be ordered on to Kingston. This leg of the march was almost easy compared to what they had been through. Le Couteur had brought his men over 1,127 kilometres (700 miles), enduring and surviving some of the worst conditions imaginable. It had been an ordeal of epic proportions.

The War of 1812 was about to enter its next phase, and the 104th Foot, raised in New Brunswick, was needed to help defend Upper Canada (Ontario).

Le Couteur, a native of Jersey, the largest of the Channel Islands, had been born in 1794 and graduated from the British Royal Military College in 1810. Two years later, after gaining the rank of lieutenant in the 104th Foot, he sailed for Canada to join his regiment. He arrived at Halifax on June 21, 1812. Five days later he learned that on June 18 the United States had declared war on Great Britain. Le Couteur journeyed on to Fredericton where the 104th was garrisoned, and remained there until the winter march of early 1813 took him to Kingston.

After further garrison duty there, the 104th was ordered to join the army fighting in the Niagara Peninsula, arriving there in mid-June 1813.

On July 25, 1814, he and his regiment fought in the Battle of Lundy's Lane which took place in and around the area of present-day Drummond Hill Cemetery in Niagara Falls. Here, in a five-hour night battle, some 3,600 British and Canadian soldiers faced 2,800 U.S. troops. It was the most stubbornly fought and bloodiest battle of the war.

Around midnight, the Americans withdrew to their camp at Chippawa, leaving the British in possession of the field. Le Couteur wrote: "I was on duty that night. What a dismal night. There were 300 dead on the Niagara side of the hill, and about 100 of ours, besides several hundred wounded. The miserable badly wounded were groaning and imploring us for water.... The scene of the morning was not more pleasant than the night's horrors. We had to wait on our slaughter-house till 11 before we got a mouthful – when a great camp kettle of thick chocolate revived us surprisingly, though we devoured it among dead bodies in all directions."

As the war continued that year, Le Couteur got to know much of the Niagara Peninsula. He took part in the British assault on American-held Fort Erie on August 15, 1814. Here he miraculously escaped with his life after a powder magazine blew up during the attack, killing hundreds of men. He was stationed at various times in Chippawa, Queenston and Fort George. On October 20, he was in the last local action of the war at the Battle of Cook's Mills, about 16 kilometres (10 miles) west of Niagara Falls.

During his time here, however, there were also moments for diversion. For example, on July 30, 1814, five days after the Battle of Lundy's Lane, he and a friend viewed Niagara Falls from Table Rock. On September 23, the young officer met some friends at Rorback's Inn (now the Whirlpool House at the corner of Portage Road and Church's Lane in Niagara Falls) where they had "a capital dinner and a bottle of port." While stationed at Queenston, he and a companion went fishing in the gorge just below the Whirlpool. It was a short trip, however, since they were soon fired on by an American rifleman stationed on the opposite side of the river.

Following the war, Le Couteur was stationed in Montreal and Quebec City. The 104th Foot was dissolved in May 1817, and he returned to England. Resigning his commission the following year, Le Couteur went back home to Jersey where,

shortly after, he married his cousin, Harriet. He spent the rest of his life devoted to public service, promoting the welfare of the island in every possible way. In 1830, he was made Jersey militia aide-de-camp to King William IV and continued these duties under Queen Victoria. In recognition of his long and extraordinary service, he was knighted in 1872. Colonel Sir John Le Couteur died on Christmas Eve, 1875. He was 81 years old.

In 1895, the Canadian federal government erected this memorial in Drummond Hill Cemetery, Niagara Falls, site of the Battle of Lundy's Lane, July 25, 1814. It honours those who fought and died in this bloody conflict during the War of 1812.

Photo by Sherman Zavitz.

Alexander McMullen: "Scenes of Horror"

An artist's interpretation of the bloody Battle of Lundy's Lane, where Alexander McMullen fought valiantly and lived to tell of the horror of war.

Niagara Falls History Museum, Niagara Falls, Ontario.

On February 20, 1814, Governor Simon Snyder of Pennsylvania ordered a draft of 1,000 men from four counties to help augment the American militia. It was during the War of 1812, and the United States had hopes that 1814 would see a final, successful invasion of Canada that would end the war in its favour.

Alexander McMullen, aged 23, was one of a hundred men from Franklin County who answered the call. Over the next few months his courage and endurance would be tested beyond his wildest imagination, and death would stare at him straight in the eye.

From McMullen's narrative, written a few years after the conflict, we can get a fascinating picture of what one man's experience was like as an American soldier during the War of 1812.

The quotas from various parts of the state gradually came together and by March 16, when they were camped at Pittsburgh, the regiment had been formed. Then began a ten-day march "through a deep snow and swampy roads" to Erie, Pennsylvania.

Here dissatisfaction began due to the poor food – moldy flour along with beef and pork that was unfit to be eaten. A number of men tried to desert, but were captured and brought back to the camp.

In early May, McMullen volunteered to join a large raiding party that was about to cross Lake Erie to the Canadian side. On May 15 he was one of the soldiers ordered to put the torch to the settlement of Dover Mills near present-day Port Dover, Ontario. Later, he wrote, "a beautiful village, which the sun shone on in splendour that morning, was before two o'clock a heap of smoking ruins." The troops then set sail back across the lake to Erie.

Soon after, the regiment made an eight-day march to Buffalo to join the Grand Army of some 5,000 men, under the command of Major-General Jacob Brown.

All through June the men were trained into fighting form under the watchful eye of Brigadier General Winfield Scott. They rose at four o'clock, had roll call, drilled for one hour, ate breakfast, drilled another four hours, broke over the noon hour and then drilled again in the afternoon.

Finally, the moment came for the invasion of Canada to begin. During the early morning hours of July 3, a vast American force crossed the Niagara River. Fort Erie soon surrendered. The following day the American troops marched north along the Niagara River towards Chippawa where the British held the strategic bridge over Chippawa Creek.

On July 5, Alexander McMullen took part in the Battle of Chippawa, fought just south of the village near the Niagara River. Phineas Riall, the British commander, decided to advance and launch an attack on the American position, but soon found himself overwhelmed by enemy fire power and forced to retreat to the Chippawa Creek bridge. McMullen wrote: "A number of killed or wounded lay on the plains where the army had fought. We marched past them towards the bridge, saluted by the cannon balls from the British works at Chippawa." It was a decisive American victory. Riall later retreated all the way to Fort George.

Twenty days later, on July 25, McMullen found himself in the thick of the action at the Battle of Lundy's Lane, fought in and around the area of what is now Drummond Hill Cemetery in Niagara Falls, Ontario. During the height of this evening battle, some 2,800 American troops and 3,600 British and Canadians fought the most desperate battle of the war.

The British and Canadians were defending the top of the hill where Drummond Hill Presbyterian Church now stands. While attempting to force their way up that hill, McMullen and his fellow soldiers found that "showers of musket balls came over our heads like a sweeping hail storm. In our march we passed over the dead and dying who were literally in heaps."

McMullen and his brigade advanced a short distance, but were soon forced to retreat under heavy fire. He sensed his own death was very near: "I felt my situation to be an awful one, and I did sincerely wish that the British army, who were on the hill in view of us, might not come down to commence the engagement again."

Around midnight, with both exhausted armies having fought each other to a standstill, the Americans withdrew to their camp at Chippawa. Alexander

McMullen, his face scorched by powder, was exhausted and almost crazed by thirst. But he had survived.

The following morning, back at the Americans' Chippawa camp, he checked a number of the tents. Nearly all of them contained one or more wounded, suffering terribly and covered in blood.

Later that same day, he came down with a high fever. Hoping to get some medical attention, he boarded one of the 42 wagons loaded with wounded heading to Fort Erie. The ride was so rough, however, that he decided to walk. But the fever had weakened him so badly that he soon lay down in front of a house, not caring whether he lived or died. A passing soldier eventually picked him up and helped him along. That night he slept in a field while the rain came down in torrents. When he awoke the following morning, still with a high fever, he was lying in about five centimetres (two inches) of water.

McMullen was finally able to make his way to a hospital in Buffalo, where, by fortitude and luck, he recovered. Of the 100 men who had left Franklin County that spring, only 25 were still alive. For Alexander McMullen, the war had shown him "scenes of horror" that he hoped, "I may never witness again."

Jarvis Hanks: Drummer Boy at the Battle of Lundy's Lane

Young Jarvis Hanks took part in the Battle of Lundy's Lane, July 25, 1814. From S.G. Goodrich, *A Pictorial History of America*.

Jarvis Hanks was only 13 years old and living with his parents in Pawlet, Vermont, when an event occurred that had a profound effect on his young life – an event that would eventually bring him to Niagara.

In the early spring of 1813, an army recruiting party came through his village seeking men to enlist for the duration of the War of 1812. Hanks became very excited about the prospect of joining the army. In an account of his life written many years later, he noted, "The pomp and splendour of a military life were vividly portrayed in my foolish imagination and produced a desire to engage in the service."

While normally too young to be considered for enlistment, Hanks had a talent the American army needed – he was a drummer. His parents gave their consent on the condition that he be employed only for recruiting service and not in battle. The officer in charge agreed, then, as Hanks was to learn, promptly forgot or ignored the promise.

After saying good-bye to his parents, an emotional episode he called "the most trying scene I had ever passed through," Hanks made his way to Rutland where the headquarters for the recruits in that area was located. His life as a drummer boy with the 11th U.S. Infantry had begun.

On April 20, the men started a march to Burlington, Vermont, and Hanks, who up to that time had enjoyed a simple but comfortable life, soon learned what it was like to devour raw pork and sleep in barns or in the open during all kinds of weather. Despite his relatively young age, however, he was something of a stoic. Mature beyond his years, his autobiography reveals that he rarely complained about the hardships and dangers of army life.

After months of training in Burlington, Hank's regiment was sent to Sacket's Harbor, New York, a military base at the eastern end of Lake Ontario. In late

October, the troops crossed the border into Canada and joined a force that eventually numbered some 4,000. The goal was to take Montreal. They were stopped by the British and Canadians at the Battle of Crysler's Farm on November 11, 1813. Here, Hanks took part in his first action.

After wintering in Fort Covington, New York, Hanks and his regiment joined thousands of other soldiers at Buffalo. This large force was commanded by Major General Jacob Brown. There followed an extensive training period under Brigadier General Winfield Scott, whom Hanks describes as "the most thorough disciplinarian I ever saw."

In the early hours of July 3, 1814, Scott led the American invasion force across the Niagara River. Fort Erie surrendered almost immediately. Hanks became so tired during this action that he "slept while marching and standing still."

Two days later came the Battle of Chippawa, a decisive American victory. The British and Canadians retreated to Fort George and the U.S. forces followed. While spending several days at Queenston, Hanks went swimming a number of times in the Niagara River. The teenager describes how he would "jump out of the third storey of a warehouse, which was 25 or 30 feet above the water, and over a wharf of 12 feet in width. It is surprising I was not killed or drowned." Deciding not to attack Fort George, the Americans moved back to Chippawa Creek.

On July 25, Jarvis Hanks took part in the Battle of Lundy's Lane, which was fought in and around what is now Drummond Hill Cemetery in Niagara Falls, Ontario. Mainly a nighttime battle, it was the fiercest and bloodiest of the war. During the opening stages of this hard-fought action, Hanks had a narrow escape. Just off the Portage Road, he found that he had to climb over a rail fence that separated a wooded area from the open battlefield. The British and Canadians, who were on the high point of ground where Drummond Hill Presbyterian Church now stands, were pouring a deadly fire on the Americans below. During the few seconds Hanks was on top of the fence, musket balls "cut the branches of trees over my head, and on my right hand and on my left, also splintered the rails on either side and under my feet, but not so much as the hair of my head was hurt!"

The Americans were eventually able to take the hill and capture the British artillery. They held this strategic position despite repeated British attempts to retake it. Much of the fighting was at close range with the bayonet freely used.

Close to midnight, with both armies exhausted, the Americans withdrew to their camp at Chippawa. However, they left all but one of the captured artillery behind. Meeting with no resistance, the British and Canadians reoccupied the field at about 7 o'clock the following morning. Losses from the battle were extremely heavy on both sides.

Jarvis Hanks survived the horror of Lundy's Lane, as well as the British siege of Fort Erie that fall. At the war's end, he was honorably discharged, and during May of 1815 "returned home in safety to my parents." He died at the age of 59 in Cleveland, Ohio.

William Dunlop:
An Army Surgeon in the War of 1812

"War is cruel and you cannot refine it.... It is only those who have never fired a shot nor heard the shrieks and groans of the wounded who cry aloud for more blood, more vengence, more destruction."

Although these were the words of the American Civil War Union General William

Tecumseh Sherman, one who shared this sentiment during the War of 1812 was William Dunlop.

Born in Scotland, Dunlop attended Glasgow University and became assistant surgeon in the 89th Regiment of Foot. He came to Canada with his regiment in November 1813.

At daylight on July 26, 1814, he arrived at what is now Niagara-on-the-Lake just as the wounded began to arrive there from the Battle of Lundy's Lane, which had taken place the previous evening. In this desperate and bloody battle, some 3,600

Dr. William Dunlop, the British surgeon who tended to the wounded following the Battle of Lundy's Lane.

From F.S.L. Ford, *William Dunlop* (1934).

British and Canadians clashed with about 2,800 Americans in the heart of what is now Niagara Falls, Ontario. This extraordinary struggle which lasted from around 7 p.m. until nearly midnight, resulted in both sides losing approximately 800 men killed, wounded or missing in action.

Dunlop's resources were meagre to meet the huge task ahead of him. The hospital was the dilapidated Butler's Barracks. (Constructed in 1778, the building stood near what is now the corner of Melville and Ricardo Streets in Niagara-on-the-Lake.) His only help was a medical sergeant and a few local women as orderlies, while his equipment consisted of just the few surgical instruments he carried with him. He worked all through the morning as wagon after wagon carne down the Portage and River Roads. By noon, Dunlop had 220 wounded men to care for.

There were not nearly enough berths, so many had to be laid on straw on the floor. It was extremely hot and flies were everywhere. They lighted on the open wounds and laid their eggs, which meant that within a few hours the wounds were crawling with maggots. Consequently, dressings had to be replaced over and over again.

Dunlop also performed numerous amputations, partly because it was the quickest way to deal with the problem of too many wounded and not enough time to properly look after them.

For two days and nights, Dunlop never sat down. On the morning of the third day, he fell asleep on his feet with his arm around the post of one of the berths. He could not be awakened, so he was placed on the hospital floor where he slept for five hours.

During the first day, an American woman, having heard that her husband had been severely wounded, crossed the Niagara River under a flag of truce and came to look for him at Butler's Barracks.

When she witnessed the scene of suffering before her, and saw her husband writhing in agony from his wounds, she exclaimed aloud, "O that the King and President were both here this moment to see the misery their quarrels lead to, they surely would never go to war without a cause that they could give as a reason to God at the last day for thus destroying the creatures that He had made in His own image."

William Dunlop fully agreed. The woman's husband died shortly after as she cradled his head in her lap.

After about a week, most of the wounded had been sent across the lake to York (Toronto) and Dunlop was posted to Chippawa, where he looked after a medical boarding house. He had the night shift, which left him free during the day. He spent most of his free time exploring the area around the Falls, which he described as "a stupendous work of nature."

This more relaxed pace soon ended, however, as Dunlop was sent to the army camped before American-held Fort Erie. He was in the thick of the action during the British assault on the fort during the early morning hours of August 15, 1814. Carrying brandy-filled wooden canteens, Dunlop comforted those soldiers too badly wounded to be moved, and pulled others to safety.

Dr. William Dunlop, through his skill, compassion, courage, and dedication, contributed much to the British war effort at Niagara. But he was also keenly aware of the limitations and, often, the futility of his situation.

Years later he wrote, "There is hardly on the face of the earth a less enviable situation than that of an army surgeon after a battle – worn out and fatigued in body and mind, surrounded by suffering, pain and misery, much of which he knows it is not in his power to heal.... While the battle lasts these all pass unnoticed, but they come before the medical man afterwards in all their sorrow and horror. It would be a useful lesson to cold-blooded politicians to witness such a scene, if only for one hour."

Shadrach Byfield Buries His Arm 14

In 1807, Shadrach Byfield, from Wiltshire, England, enlisted in His Majesty's army. When the 18-year-old told his mother of his decision, she reacted by immediately having a stroke and died three days later. Undoubtedly, Shadrach did not consider this sad turn of events to be a particularly auspicious beginning to his military career. Nevertheless, he went ahead with his plans and over the next seven years, as a private in the 41st Regiment of Foot, fought patiently and bravely in many a battle

He saw a great deal of action during the War of 1812, including the Battle of Lundy's Lane, which took place within what is now the City of Niagara Falls, Ontario, on July 25, 1814. This vicious bloody battle took place from around 7:00 p.m. until midnight. Fought at close range, the focal point of the conflict was a hill overlooking the strategic Lundy's Lane, Portage Road intersection.

After the sun set, the hill, swathed in darkness and powder smoke, was a din of many noises: the shouting and cursing of the men, the firing of muskets, the roar of artillery, the whinnying of frightened horses and the groaning of the wounded.

The 41st Regiment led an advance midway through the action. Years later, Shadrach wrote about what happened: "Our bugle then sounded for the company to drop. A volley was then fired upon us, which killed two corporals and wounded

An early view of Fort Niagara, at the mouth of the Niagara River, below Youngstown, New York, where Shadrach Byfield laid his arm to rest.

From E.B. O'Callagan, *The Documentary History of the State of New York* (1849).

a sergeant and several of the men. The company then arose, fired and charged. The enemy quit their position; we followed and took three field pieces." Despite the success of this charge, the Americans soon recaptured these guns.

Around midnight, the Americans withdrew to their camp at Chippawa. This allowed the British and Canadians to reoccupy the field the following morning. With the coming of dawn, Shadrach was one of the detail ordered to collect the many dead on the battlefield and burn them in several huge funeral pyres.

On the morning of August 3, the 41st found itself attempting to take an enemy position at Black Rock, now part of Buffalo. During the course of the action Shadrach received a severe wound in his left arm, just below the elbow. At first, the army surgeons felt amputation would not be necessary. However, a few days later at Fort Niagara, which the British had captured the previous December, they changed their minds and decided that the arm would have to come off.

Shadrach took the decision with amazing calm, even declining to be held down during the surgery. He described the operation as "tedious and painful, but I was enabled to bear it pretty well." After his arm was dressed he was given some wine and sent to bed.

At this point he was casually informed that his amputated forearm had been thrown into the fort's dung heap. Shadrach was enraged and ordered the arm removed. He saw to it that a few boards were nailed together for a coffin and the arm placed in it. The coffin was then buried on the ramparts of Fort Niagara.

His stump healed well and a few days later he was "able to play a game of fives for a quart of rum."

Shipped back to England later in 1814, he was discharged and then returned to his hometown. However, with only one arm he was unable to work at his trade as a weaver. Then one night he had a dream. As Shadrach later recalled, "I had the form of an instrument revealed to me which would enable me to work at my trade." He drew a plan of this vision on a board and took it to a blacksmith who made the instrument for him. Using this device, he was able to get a good job with a clothier.

As the years went by, however, he must have occasionally thought of his army days and how a part of him would forever remain near the river called Niagara.

The Burning Spring: "An Object of a Good Deal of Interest"

15

"Many are very much interested and to those who have never seen anything of the kind, it is an object of a good deal of interest."

So wrote F. H. Johnson in a guidebook about Niagara Falls, published in 1867. He was referring to the Burning Spring, a well-known Niagara Falls tourist attraction for over a century.

In the 1790s while excavating for a mill in the area now known as Dufferin Islands, a natural gas "spring" was discovered.

It was learned in later years that the gas, which bubbled up through the water, was coming from a layer of Queenston Shale which runs deep underground along the upper Niagara River.

The excavators had accidentally enlarged the opening of an existing vent, allowing a rapid emission of the natural gas. This phenomenon quickly became a local curiosity.

Stereoscopic card depicting the Burning Spring as it was shown to visitors in the 1870s.

John Burtniak Collection.

Not long after the War of 1812, as tourism began to grow in Niagara Falls, some clever and enterprising individual realized that the spring had the potential to make money as an attraction for visitors.

Accordingly, a building was constructed over it. The spring was then enclosed by a barrel that had a pipe protruding from the top. A cork stopper was placed in the pipe, which caused the gas to build up pressure in the barrel. When the cork was removed, the gas was lighted and you had a "Burning Spring."

The attraction, which was located close to the Niagara River at the south end of present-day Dufferin Islands, proved to be very popular. This was partly due to the fact that, for the time, it was not only unique, but also seemed to have an aura of mystery surrounding it.

All the early Niagara guidebooks mention the Burning Spring. For example, Horatio Parsons, writing in 1836, notes the Burning Spring "is in a state of constant ebullition and from it issues a stream of sulphuretted hydrogen gas which quickly ignites on the touch of a candle and burns with a brilliant flame. The keeper of the Spring, Mr. J. Conklin, expects a small fee from visitors for his trouble."

By the early 1880s, an extra feature had been added for those who came to see the Burning Spring. As a writer of the time informed his readers, "Glasses of the gaseous water are given to visitors and are said to possess rare medicinal properties."

Around 1885, however, the Burning Spring developed a problem. It ran out of gas.

In 1887, the newly formed Niagara Parks Commission, as it is now known, expropriated the site of the Burning Spring, as well as the adjacent islands. The owner, Sutherland Macklem, was awarded $100,000.

A new, private company then constructed a Burning Spring building on top of the bank behind Dufferin Islands at the junction of Portage Road and Burning Spring Hill Road. Natural gas was piped into this new location.

While the attraction regained a measure of its former popularity, it apparently was not considered by some to be as interesting or mysterious as it had once been. Niagara Falls, New York author Peter Porter, writing about the Burning Spring in 1901, noted, "It is not worth visiting nor the payment of the admission fee."

The Burning Spring was relocated again around 1905 to a site near the junction of Portage Road and Stanley Avenue at Falls View.

Another move came in 1924 when a new building called the Falls View Observation Tower and Old Burning Spring was constructed on the high bank directly overlooking the Horseshoe Falls.

Along with the Burning Spring, this two-storey building housed a gift shop and tearoom. The "observation tower" was actually the roof from which there was a beautiful view of the Falls.

Advertising from around 1930 proclaimed, "Both Niagara Falls and the Old Burning Spring are still great attractions. All who come to Niagara should make a point of visiting Falls View and the ancient Burning Spring with its pillar of fire leaping to a height of 25 feet. Do not miss seeing this ancient wonder."

In 1962, the business, which had been operated for many years by the Langmuir family, was sold to Malcolm Howe and Arthur White. Following extensive renovations, the new owners established the Burning Spring Wax Museum in the building. While the wax displays were highlighted, the Burning Spring was still a featured part of the operation.

A disastrous fire struck the building in 1969, but repairs were made and the business resumed.

The final curtain came down, however, in 1993, when the Burning Spring Wax Museum closed and the building was demolished, thus bringing to an end a Niagara attraction that had endured for around 175 years.

Sam Patch:
Niagara's First Stunter

16

Sam Patch's claim to stunting fame at Niagara was jumping into the Niagara River from a platform he had built in front of Goat Island.

From Francis J. Petrie, *Roll Out the Barrel* (1985).

The spectators viewing Niagara Falls on Wednesday, October 7, 1829, could scarcely believe what they were seeing.

Out in front of Goat Island, which separates the American and Horseshoe Falls, was a small, specially-built platform some 28.5 metres (85 feet) above the

Niagara River. On it stood a young man who was about to jump into the water below.

The man was Sam Patch, 22 years old, from Rhode Island. He had already gained some fame two years earlier when he jumped from a bridge crossing the Passaic River in New Jersey. Now he was about to become Niagara's first stunter.

Among the crowd on hand to witness the event was William Lyon Mackenzie, who later wrote in his Toronto *Colonial Advocate* newspaper: "The celebrated Sam Patch actually leaped over the Falls of Niagara into the vast abyss below.... While the boats below were on the lookout for him he had in one minute reached the shore unnoticed and unhurt, and was heard on the beach singing as merrily as if altogether unconscious of having performed an act so extraordinary as almost to appear an incredible fable. Sam Patch has immortalized himself."

Sam, however, was not content with either the size of the audience or the money earned from his feat. Accordingly, he announced that in a few days he would perform an even higher jump. Inserting an advertisement in the *Colonial Advocate*, he explained: "Having been thus disappointed, the owners of Goat Island have generously granted me the use of it for nothing so that I may have a chance from an equally generous public to obtain some remuneration for my long journey hither, as well as affording me an opportunity for supporting the reputation I have gained by aeronautical feats never before attempted either in the Old or New World."

Sam made his second jump on Saturday, October 17, 1829. At exactly 3 p.m., he leaped into the Niagara River from the incredible height of 39 metres (130 feet). Miraculously, he again survived.

He then decided to move his act to the Genesee Falls near Rochester, New York. Here it was proclaimed that on Friday, November 13, he would make a leap of 36 metres (120 feet) and that it would be "Sam's last jump." It turned out to be just that. His body wasn't recovered until the following spring when it was located in the lower reaches of the Genesee River, near the village of Charlotte.

Sam Patch, Niagara's first stunter, had made one too many jumps.

Fanny Trollope: "Wonder, Terror and Delight"

17

Fanny Trollope was no ordinary woman for her time. As a young wife and mother living in nineteenth century England, she was not expected to do anything more than manage her household and raise her children. But this kind of life was too confining for Fanny.

Born Francis Milton, she married lawyer Thomas Trollope in 1809 when she was 29. In 1827, after her husband's career had been faltering for several years, she packed her trunks, took three of their six children (a son and two daughters) and headed for the United States to seek her fortune.

After reaching New Orleans, she headed for Nashoba, a racially integrated community in Tennessee that she had heard about where work

MRS TROLLOPE

Fanny Trollope, a noted nineteenth-century visitor to Niagara Falls, published a colourful description of her American tour in 1832.

From *The National Portrait Gallery of Illustrious and Eminent Personages.*

was shared and communal living was practised. After only a few weeks there, however, Fanny realized that this was not the type of life for her or her children. She moved on to the Mississippi and Ohio Rivers, eventually reaching Cincinnati.

Here she remained for over a year during which time she managed to have a large building constructed and open what she called a bazaar that sold goods she imported from England. The idea was to "civilize" the Americans.

The business failed, with the locals deriding it as "Trollope's Folly ."

Undaunted, Fanny and her children continued their travels, spending time in such places as Wheeling, Washington, Philadelphia and New York. She was a careful observer who loved to write and so was constantly recording her impressions of people and places in her journals.

During June of 1831, Fanny and her two daughters (her son had returned to England on his own) reached Niagara Falls. It was a moment she had dreamed about and wrote, "It was the brightest day June could give, and almost any day would have seemed bright that brought me to the object which for years I had languished to look upon."

They checked into the Pavilion Hotel, which overlooked the Falls from where the Oakes Hotel now stands. Anxious to view the famous cataract, Fanny and her daughters ran to the upper gallery of the hotel, so excited that, as she wrote, "I trembled like a fool, and my girls clung to me trembling too, but with faces beaming with delight." Fanny's first look at the Falls immediately convinced her that the sight was "all I had wished for, hoped for, dreamed of. I can only say that wonder, terror and delight completely overwhelmed me."

She noted that many visitors arrived at the hotel in the morning, walked to the Falls, returned to the hotel for dinner and then left by the evening coach. Fanny was determined, however, to see everything and fully experience Niagara Falls. As a result, she and her daughters spent four days here. In her journal she recorded, "We drenched ourselves in spray; we cut our feet on the rocks; we blistered our faces in the sun; we looked up the cataract and down the cataract; we perched ourselves on every pinnacle we could find; we dipped our fingers in the flood at a few yards' distance from its thundering fall; in short, we strove to fill as many niches of memory with Niagara as possible; I think that the images will be within the power of recall forever."

The Trollopes returned to England and to the rest of their family in July 1831. Fanny used the copious notes she had made during her travels to develop a book entitled *Domestic Manners of the Americans*. Published the following year, it was a great success and launched her career as a best-selling author. Over the next 24 years she had another 40 books published, including both novels and travelogues. Rising every day at four in the morning, she would then write for about three hours.

While spending some of her time in England, Fanny also began to enjoy extended stays in various cities on the Continent. She died on October 6, 1863, while living in Florence, Italy, and was buried in the English cemetery there. Through her talent, energy, ingenuity and independent spirit, Fanny Trollope made a significant contribution to the literary world of her day.

William Lyon Mackenzie: Flight to the Border

18

On Thursday, December 7, 1837, a remarkable scene took place near the intersection of Yonge and St. Clair Streets near Toronto. In what was then a rural area, 150 rebels, led by William Lyon Mackenzie, clashed with around 900 government militia. It was no contest. The rebels were not only outnumbered, but were also short on military training and arms. In 20 minutes they had been scattered in all directions.

The aim of these rebels, and many other sympathizers in what is now southern Ontario, was to bring about a government more responsible to the people. An extreme group had finally decided that the use of force was the only way to achieve this goal.

A portrait of William Lyon Mackenzie.

From Charles Lindsey, *The Life and Times of Wm. Lyon Mackenzie* (1862).

Knowing he would be charged with treason if captured, Mackenzie fled for the Niagara River where he could cross into the United States. That night he slept in a farmhouse. The following morning, in company with the farmer's 19-year-old son, Alan Wilcox, he made it to the Oakville area. Since the bridge over the Sixteen Mile Creek here was guarded, the two men were forced to ford the waterway. Mackenzie later wrote, "We accordingly stripped ourselves naked, and with the surface ice beating against us, and holding our garments over our heads, in a bitterly cold December night, buffeted the current, and were soon up to our necks.... The cold in that stream caused me the most cruel and intense sensation of pain I ever endured... and the frozen sand on the bank seemed to warm our feet when we once more trod on it."

After a night at another friend's home, Mackenzie left Wilcox, who was suffering from exposure, and continued on his way alone, constantly on the alert for government troops. By Sunday afternoon he had reached Smithville, some 40 kilometres (25 miles) from the border. There he met a rebel sympathizer by the name of Samuel Chandler who offered to help him reach the Niagara River. Chandler was a wagon maker from the then-bustling community of St. Johns, located in the Short Hills, just north of present-day Fonthill.

Mackenzie and Chandler rode out of Smithville and headed east. According to some accounts, they went to St. Johns, where they had dinner in Chandler's home. (A stone marker in St. Johns now identifies the location of the house.)

The two horsemen then rode on into the cold night. They crossed the Welland Canal at Allanburg and possibly stopped at the nearby Black Horse Inn, which stood on the southwest corner of what is now the Highway No. 20 and Allanport Road intersection. The inn was managed by Ira Stimson, another Mackenzie supporter and son-in-law of John Wilson, whose farm home in Crowland, near Cooks Mills, was their next objective.

They arrived at Wilson's before daylight on Monday morning, December 11. A sleigh was provided to take the men the final 21 kilometres (13 miles) to the Niagara River, although it was not driven right to the road along the river for fear of detection by troops patrolling the border. So the final portion was done on foot.

Mackenzie and Chandler walked into rebel sympathizer Samuel McAfee's riverside home about nine o'clock. A large breakfast was prepared for them, but before sitting down to eat Mackenzie decided to make a check outside. To his horror he saw in the distance a detachment of dragoons "with carbines at the ready" coming down the road.

McAfee, with Mackenzie and Chandler helping, quickly hauled his boat across the road. They had just launched it, and were a little way out from the riverbank, when the troops rode up to the house. Mackenzie later noted, "How we escaped here, is to me almost a miracle.... A boat was in the river, against official orders... not a few men must have seen the whole movement, and yet we were allowed to steer for the head of Grand Island with all the expedition in our power.... In an hour we were safe on the American shore." (A plaque along the upper Niagara Parkway marks the site of the crossing.)

Mackenzie remained in the United States until he was pardoned in 1849. He returned to Toronto the following year where he lived until his death in 1861. By this time responsible government had long since been achieved by more peaceful means.

Samuel Chandler had gone back to Canada where he was arrested for treason in 1838. He was sentenced to hang, but this was changed to exile in Van Diemen's Land (Tasmania). Escaping from there in 1842, Chandler went to live in Iowa where he died in 1866.

Historical plaque marking "Mackenzie's Crossing," on the upper Niagara River. Photo by Sherman Zavitz

The Pavilion: Niagara Falls' First Great Hotel

19

The Pavilion, Niagara's first major hotel, overlooked the Falls of Niagara.
From Kiwanis Club of Stamford, Ontario, Inc., *Niagara Falls, Canada; A History of the City* (1967).

If you had come to see the famous Falls of Niagara during the 1820s or 1830s, chances are good that you would have stayed at the Pavilion Hotel.

During those decades, when tourism here was just beginning, it was the most popular and far-famed hotel in the area. Built in 1822 by William Forsyth, the Pavilion stood at Fallsview (originally spelled Falls View) where the Oakes Hotel now stands.

Forsyth was one of Niagara's earliest entrepreneurs in the tourism industry. As early as 1819, he was operating an inn on the same site where he later built the Pavilion. He also operated a stage coach line along the Portage Road and had some involvement with the ferry service that crossed the Niagara River below the Falls.

The Pavilion was three storeys high and of white clapboard construction. At both the front, which faced Portage Road, and the back, which overlooked the Falls, were galleries for viewing the area's scenery. On the pillars, which supported these galleries, many guests would leave messages written in pencil – possibly Niagara's first graffiti. There was also a lookout area on the roof. Horatio Parson's guidebook of 1836 noted, "The Pavilion has an imposing appearance, and from the observatory on its roof visitors have an extensive view of the surrounding country."

Adam Fergusson, of Scotland, visited Niagara in 1831. Arriving opposite the Falls, he noted, "A splendid and extensive establishment was soon after recognized as Forsyth's hotel." At the Pavilion's popular bar, he met well-known Upper Canada frontiersman, Dr. William "Tiger" Dunlop. This was the same Dr. Dunlop who had tended many of the British and Canadian wounded following the Battle of Lundy's Lane. (See Story 13).

Fergusson wrote, "I scarce recollect of anything more welcome than a beverage with which my companion regaled me at Forsyth's, under some odd name, but which consisted of a bottle of good brown stout turned into a quart of iced water, with a sufficient quantity of ginger, cinnamon and sugar; truly it was a prescription worthy of being filled."

In 1827, William Forsyth, in an attempt to counter increasing competition in the hotel and tourist business, made a bold and, as he found out, illegal move. When the earliest surveys were done in this area, a reserve of one chain (20 metres or 50 feet) in width was made along the west (Canadian) bank of the Niagara River. This was held by the government, mainly for military purposes. Table Rock and the Horseshoe Falls, focal points for most visitors, were directly below the Pavilion, so Forsyth decided to erect a high rail fence enclosing that part of the Chain Reserve abutting his property. The public no longer had free access to the Falls, except for those he allowed to go through his premises.

This action, quite naturally, brought howls of protest. The government ordered Forsyth to remove the offending fence. He refused. The Lieutenant-Governor then sent in a detachment of soldiers who knocked it down and in the process also destroyed some of Forsyth's crops and his blacksmith shop. The fence was rebuilt and again removed by troops. Forsyth launched two civil suits against the government. He lost both.

Discouraged, Forsyth sold the Pavilion Hotel in 1832 and moved to what is now Fort Erie. There, he eventually built a new home. Known as Bertie Hall, this imposing structure still stands along the Niagara Boulevard. Forsyth needed a big house wherever he went, since he had 19 children, 10 by his first wife and nine by his second.

During the mid-1830s, the Pavilion began a decline in popularity. The end came on the freezing night of February 19, 1839, when it was destroyed in a spectacular fire. Samuel DeVeaux, who lived in what is now Niagara Falls, New York, was an eyewitness and wrote this vivid account: "It continued burning for some time in the evening. The spectacle was grand and solemn. The building was very large and composed entirely of wood. The light reflected upon the rising spray from the Falls, and upon the trees covered with concealed ice. The cloud of mist appeared like another conflagration, and to persons at a distance was taken to be such. The ice on the trees reflected back the blazing light, and shone brilliantly in the keen, pure air like burning coal. Though thus dazzling yet it was a sad and painful sight."

Andrew Drew: The Destruction of the *Caroline*

20

At around 10 p.m. on the bitterly cold night of December 29, 1837, seven long-boats, each containing eight men armed with cutlass and pistol, quietly slipped into the Niagara River at Chippawa.

The steamboat *Caroline*, in flames and breaking up, floats to its doom just above the Horseshoe Falls, December 29, 1837.

From J.E. Middleton, *The Romance of Ontario* (1931).

Embarking on a daring mission, the little expedition was headed for the eastern side of Navy Island.

As the men pulled on their muffled oars, they no doubt thought about the reason they were steering for this small Canadian-owned island in the Niagara River, about 4.8 kilometres (three miles) above the Falls. Their objective was to search out and capture a steamboat of some 42 tonnes (40 tons) known as the *Caroline*.

Seated in the lead boat was the man in charge of the expedition, Commander Andrew Drew. A well-respected, popular and seasoned naval officer, Drew must have recalled with considerable satisfaction how only hours before he had appealed for volunteers to join this dangerous exploit. There was an immediate and overwhelming response – many of the men declaring that they would be willing to follow the commander "to the devil" if need be.

As he peered ahead into the blackness, Drew might well have also reflected on the many events in his active life that had brought him to this moment.

Born in London, England, in 1792, he joined the Royal Navy at the age of 14. With Britain then at war with Napoleon, Drew was soon involved with the work of a wartime navy. He took part, for example, in the attack on Boulogne, the bombardment of Copenhagen and in blockade operations off the coast of Spain.

During an action against the French frigate *La Clorinde* on February 24, 1814, Drew displayed such gallantry that he was later promoted to lieutenant. Another advancement came in 1824 when, following his brilliant defense of a castle on the west African coast, he was made a commander.

Shortly after this, however, Drew found himself out of a job. Following Napoleon's defeat in 1815, the navy had been gradually reducing the size of its active fleet, which meant it no longer needed as many commissioned officers. As a result, like many other men in the same situation, Drew became a half pay officer – still on the active list but laid off.

For nearly eight years he languished, hoping to be recalled to duty. With considerable regret, he finally decided that his naval career was finished and that it was time to get on with his life. He then accepted a job opportunity that would require him to go to Upper Canada (Ontario) where he would receive at no cost to himself, a partnership in a potentially valuable property. Shortly after his marriage to Mary Henderson on March 17, 1832, Drew and his bride embarked for Canada.

They settled in Blandford Township on the present site of Woodstock, Ontario – in fact, Drew and his partner, Henry Vansittart, are considered the co-founders of that community. For the next five years, he happily busied himself in managing and expanding both his private and the partnership's interests.

Then came the Rebellion of 1837. For a number of years there had been mounting agitation on the part of many people, especially in the rural areas, for government reform in Upper Canada.

The situation turned violent on December 7, 1837, when an armed force of radical reformers under the leadership of William Lyon Mackenzie marched on Toronto. They were quickly routed by government troops, forcing Mackenzie to flee with a price on his head. Four days later, after a harrowing journey through the Niagara Peninsula, he crossed the Niagara River to safety in the United States.

On December 14, Mackenzie, along with other refugees from the rebellion and a number of American sympathizers, occupied and then began to fortify Navy Island. They set up a provisional government there and over the next several weeks, as the number of recruits increased, made plans to invade the Upper Canada mainland.

To deal with this crisis, a large force of militia from the Hamilton area under the command of Colonel Allan MacNab was sent to Chippawa to augment the local militia already on duty there. MacNab had also been authorized to raise a naval brigade and selected Commander Andrew Drew to lead this force. Although MacNab wanted to attack Navy Island, he had been ordered to take only a defensive position – something that rankled him as well as Drew.

However, events were about to take a decisive turn.

On December 28, the *Caroline*, which the rebels had leased from her Buffalo owner, began to operate as a supply ship, travelling back and forth between Navy Island and Fort Schlosser, which was opposite the island on the American mainland.

Through his spies, MacNab was made aware of the *Caroline's* activities that same day.

He was infuriated and on the following afternoon, despite his orders, asked Drew if he could "cut out that boat." Drew's reply was, "Nothing easier." MacNab then simply said, "Do it!"

So it was that as midnight approached on December 29, 1837, Drew and his men approached the eastern side of Navy Island.

The men were tense, realizing that they could be spotted by rebel sentries at any moment. Not only was Navy Island known to be fortified, but a barrier consisting of tree branches that extended from the shoreline to open water had been placed around the island. This would make it difficult for an invasion force to make a landing.

Chagrined at not finding the *Caroline* anchored off the island, Drew realized that it must be at Fort Schlosser. Deciding to make his way there, Drew and his men quietly rowed on through the darkness. Their objective soon came in sight. Maneuvering their longboats through the shadows, the men managed to get to within about 30 metres (100 feet) of the steamboat before a lone armed guard spotted them. He demanded the password. Drew reportedly answered, "I shall give it to you when I get on board." Not satisfied with that reply, the guard yelled for the crew members who were sleeping below deck and then fired – the shot narrowly missing Drew's head.

Within seconds, the raiders had snatched their grappling pikes, seized the *Caroline* at several points and, pistols and cutlasses at the ready, boarded her. A short but sharp skirmish followed as Drew and his men kicked in the doors of the sleeping quarters and began to drive the crew and others on board off the ship and onto the wharf. Several of the raiders were wounded during the encounter. One of them, named Reynolds, managed to grab his assailant with one hand and, throwing him down, "knocked his brains out with the butt end of my pistol."

The *Caroline* was soon secured and cleared of all those who had been on board. Deciding that it would take too long to get up steam and take the vessel to Chippawa under its own power, Drew ordered that the boat be set on fire. Accordingly, as it was being towed away from the wharf, some blankets in the ladies' cabin were soaked in oil and then torched.

Cut loose, the doomed ship was soon caught in the current and now, fully engulfed in flames, heading downstream towards the Falls. A militiaman who had taken part in the ship's capture later wrote, "It was a splendid sight which shed a light for many miles around."

Most of the *Caroline* broke up and sank in the Upper Rapids. Only a few parts actually went over the Falls. (One of these was the figurehead which was later found near Lewiston and is now in the Buffalo and Erie County Historical Society's collection.)

Commander Drew and all of his men made it safely back to Chippawa. They were guided by a huge bonfire that was set at the mouth of Chippawa Creek to act as a beacon. Drew estimated that five or six of his opponents had been killed during the skirmish. In fact, however, only one man had lost his life.

The *Caroline* incident immediately ignited passions on both sides of the border with the result that tensions ran high for a number of months. Canadians were elated at what had happened, proclaiming Drew along with his crew and MacNab as heroes.

Americans were incensed that Canadian troops had invaded United States territory and destroyed both property and life. The fact that the *Caroline* was involved in an illegal activity and that Mackenzie's many American supporters had helped to seize Canadian-owned Navy Island was not, apparently, taken into account.

For a number of days after the *Caroline's* destruction there was heavy firing back and forth across the Niagara River between the rebels (or Patriots as they called themselves) on Navy Island and Canadian militia on the mainland. Three militiamen were killed, including a naval gunner at Chippawa who was struck in the leg with a cannonball. He died several hours after his leg was amputated.

During this time, some Americans urged President Van Buren to declare war on Great Britain and Canada. Fortunately, he supported peace and neutrality. The situation was somewhat defused when the Patriots and their sympathizers evacuated Navy Island on January 14, 1838.

In the meantime, those who had taken part in the *Caroline* expedition found themselves marked men since they now faced retaliation from the Patriots. Apparently Drew himself did not escape. One account states that during November 1838, nearly a year after the boat's destruction, an attempt was made on his life while he was staying with the Cummings family at their Chippawa home.

Drew had hoped for a promotion as a reward for his successful leadership in the *Caroline* affair. However, the British government felt that it would be unwise to reward him while at the same time it was trying to soothe American feelings over the incident.

Nevertheless, Drew was kept on active deity and in the fall of 1838, was asked to organize and lead a Provincial Marine.

Even though he had become one of the province's most prominent individuals, Drew, along with his wife and the couple's six children, left Canada during the summer of 1842, and moved back to England. Supposedly he had reason to believe that by returning there his naval career would be advanced.

This turned out to be true since late that same year he was given command of a ship on duty in the Caribbean. His longed-for promotion to Captain finally came during the fall of 1843, following his return to England.

While he never commanded at sea again, Drew did serve as naval storekeeper at a post near Cape Town, South Africa, from 1850 to 1863. During this time, he was promoted again, first to Rear Admiral and then Admiral. Undoubtedly, this brought immense satisfaction to Drew, who many years before was convinced that his career in the navy was finished. That this turned out to not be the case was due in large measure to a little steamboat on the Niagara River called the *Caroline*.

Admiral Andrew Drew RN died at his home in England on December 19, 1878, at the age of 86.

Benjamin Lett:
A Terrorist at Niagara

21

At around 2 a.m. on November 16, 1838, Captain Edgeworth Ussher, his wife Sally and the couple's four children were asleep in their home, which stood along the Niagara River just south of Chippawa.

Suddenly the night silence was shattered by a loud knock at the door. Despite protests from his wife, Ussher lit a candle and went to investigate. As he reached the door, two shots rang out of the blackness, leaving Edgeworth Ussher slumped on his doorstep, a dead man.

The year 1838 was a troubled one in what is now southern Ontario. Eleven months

A sketch from 1842 showing the original Brock's Monument after it was damaged by an explosion, apparently perpetrated by Benjamin Lett two years earlier.

From James C. Moren, *Historical Monuments and Observations of Lundy's Lane and Queenston Heights* (1929).

before Ussher's murder, an armed revolt against the government had taken place just north of Toronto. Most were fighting for constitutional reform, although some extremists wanted to rid Canada completely of British rule. The rebellion was quickly crushed and many of the protesters fled to the United States side of the Niagara River. From here some of these men, calling themselves Patriots, began to carry out terrorist activities on Canadian soil.

Captain Ussher was well known along the Niagara Frontier for his loyalty to Britain and his hatred of the Patriots. This had made him a marked man. The prime suspect in his murder was a Patriot named Benjamin Lett, and the government soon offered a reward for his capture.

Lett and his family had come to Canada from Ireland in 1819, when he was five years old. The family eventually settled on a farm along Lake Ontario just east of Toronto.

Benjamin's hatred of the British apparently stemmed from an incident in 1837 when a band of local Orangemen shot at him for refusing to join an expedition to hunt down rebels opposed to the government. This action brought him into the Patriot forces at Niagara.

Ussher's assassination was not the only crime in which Lett became implicated. In January 1839, he made an unsuccessful attempt to burn a British ship at Kingston. Six months later he was involved in a failed raid on the town of Cobourg. On April 17, 1840, an explosion of gunpowder largely destroyed the original Brock's Monument at Queenston Heights. Officials were sure Lett was primarily responsible for the vandalism. In June of the same year, he attempted to burn a steamship at Oswego, New York. This led to his arrest by American troops.

Convicted of arson, Lett was sentenced to seven years of hard labour at the Auburn, New York, prison. However, while being escorted there, he managed to get away from his guards, jump down a 6-metre (20-foot) embankment and escape into some woods.

The governor of New York immediately offered a reward for his recapture. Lett was described as "5 ft. 11 inches high, rather slim, sandy hair and whiskers, very red faced and freckled, light skinned, very large, muscular hands, with round, long, and very white fingers." He was usually armed with four pistols and a Bowie knife.

After a year as a fugitive, Lett was captured in Buffalo during September 1841. Taken to the Auburn prison, he was thrown into solitary confinement. According to his brother, Thomas, the guards frequently mistreated him. Four years later, his health broken, Lett was pardoned by New York Governor Silas Wright. He then went to live with his brothers and sisters on a farm near Northville, Illinois.

On December 1, 1858, while involved in a trading expedition on Lake Michigan, he was suddenly taken ill. Carried by steamer to Milwaukee, he died there nine days later. An autopsy showed death was due to strychnine poisoning. Thomas Lett was sure government agents were responsible, and the inscription he placed on his brother's tombstone reflected his feelings about Benjamin's treatment at the hands of American authorities. It read, "The records of American partnership in the case of Benjamin Lett – they are like a Christian hell without a Jesus Christ: No escape."

"Enchanting Ground:" Charles Dickens At Niagara

22

Charles Dickens is not only one of the world's most widely read novelists, he was also one of Niagara Falls' greatest admirers. The famous writer was here in late April and early May of 1842 as part of a North American tour.

With him was his wife, Kate, and her maid, Anne. Thanks to various letters he wrote from Niagara Falls as well as a book he authored entitled

This sketch of Charles Dickens standing on Table Rock first appeared in the *Buffalo Courier* in 1912, the centennial of the famous author's birth. It is a copy of a drawing of the Horseshoe Falls made in 1842, combined with a daguerreotype of Dickens taken during his visit here that same year. From Edward T. Williams, *Scenic and Historic Niagara Falls* (1925).

American Notes for General Circulation, we know something about his impressions and experiences during the visit.

The thirty-year old Dickens was full of anticipation as he rode the train from Buffalo to Niagara Falls, New York, commenting, "I never in my life was in such a state of excitement." At the end of the two-hour journey he jumped from the train and observed "two great white clouds rising up slowly, and majestically from the depths of the earth."

Rushing down a "deep and slippery path leading to the ferry boat," the trio was then rowed over to the Canadian side. (It would be another six years before a bridge was built across the Niagara.) About half way across the river, Dickens, surveying the magnificent scene spread out before him, exclaimed, "Great God! How could any man be disappointed in this!"

They checked into the Clifton House Hotel, which stood where Oakes Garden Theatre is now located. Built in 1833, the Clifton was the most prominent hotel in Niagara Falls for over 60 years. Dickens described it as "a large, square house standing on a bold height, with overhanging eaves like a Swiss Cottage; and a wide, handsome gallery outside every story."

He was pleased with both the accommodation and, naturally, the view, writing, "Our sitting room is on the second floor and is so close to the Falls that the windows are always wet and dim with spray. Two bedrooms open out of it; one our own, one Anne's. From these chambers you can see the Falls rolling and tumbling and roaring and leaping all day long."

During the nine days he was here, Dickens carefully explored the entire area around the Horseshoe Falls, taking both day and night walks. He called it "enchanting ground."

Standing at the base of the Falls, he was moved emotionally and spiritually: "There was a bright rainbow at my feet and from that I looked up to a fall of bright green water. It would be hard for a man to stand nearer God than he does there."

Like many visitors over the years, Dickens felt that the grandest view of Niagara Falls was from Table Rock. As he wrote, "When I had looked at the great Horseshoe Falls for a few minutes from this point I comprehended the whole scene." Describing the Falls as a "tremendous spectacle," the sight created within him a feeling of what he called "peaceful eternity."

Not only did Dickens and Kate delight in the scenery here, but they were also pleased to have some time to relax and be informal. In a letter written from the Clifton House on April 29, 1842, Dickens notes, "There is no company here – to our unspeakable delight. We have the Falls to ourselves; ramble about all day long; do just as we please; play cribbage at nights; dine at two in the day; wear our oldest clothes; walk ankle-deep in the mud; and thoroughly enjoy ourselves."

Summing up their Niagara visit, Dickens felt it was "nine days of perfect repose and where we were most comfortable and happy."

However, Kate's maid, Anne, was totally unimpressed. Her only comment about the Falls was: "It's nothing but water and too much of that!"

Mark Twain: A Master Humourist Experiences Niagara

23

"Niagara Falls is a most enjoyable place of resort. The hotels are excellent and the prices not at all exorbitant."

This observation was made by the famous American author and humorist Mark Twain in an article of his entitled, "Niagara." Originally appearing in the *Buffalo Express*, it was one of a number of Twain's essays published in 1875 in book form under the title *Sketches Old and New*.

The creator of Tom Sawyer, Huckleberry Finn and many other memorable characters, Twain probably visited Niagara Falls a number of times since from February 1870 to October 1871 he lived in nearby Buffalo where he was an editor and part owner of the *Express*.

An astute observer with a well-developed wit, Twain, whose real name was Samuel Clemens, offered a number of comments about various aspects of his

Master humourist Mark Twain, seen here in 1883, had plenty to say about Niagara Falls.

Sherman Zavitz Collection.

Niagara experience. For example, he mentions climbing down a 45-metre (148-foot) staircase to stand by the edge of the river and then observes, "After you have done it, you will wonder why you did it; but you will then be too late."

After paying an admission fee, he listened to a guide relate, "in his blood-curdling way," how he saw the *Maid of the Mist* piloted downriver through the Whirlpool Rapids to Queenston on June 6, 1861. Twain noted "She did finally live through the trip after accomplishing the incredible feat of travelling seventeen miles in six minutes or six miles in seventeen minutes, I have really forgotten which." (If I may be permitted, Mr. Twain, it was the latter. SZ)

Twain felt it was "worth the price of admission to hear the guide tell the story nine times in succession to different parties and never miss a word or alter a sentence or gesture."

He crossed over the Suspension Bridge to view the Falls from the Canadian side. The bridge, an engineering marvel of its time, stood where the Whirlpool Rapids Bridge is now located. It was a double-deck span with trains using the upper level, while the lower deck was for carriages and pedestrians.

Twain found (or pretended to find) the crossing to be disconcerting, writing, "You drive over the Suspension Bridge and divide your misery between the chances of smashing down 200 feet into the river below, and the chances of having the railway train overhead smashing down on you. Either possibility is discomforting taken by itself, but mixed together, they amount in the aggregate to positive unhappiness."

As his carriage approached the Horseshoe Falls, which he described as "stupendous," Twain, was surprised and somewhat upset to find "long ranks of photographers standing guard behind their cameras."

Back on the American side, he took the Cave of the Winds trip – a popular experience still today with visitors. As he crept along the footbridges built over the rocks at the foot of the American Falls, Twain was awed by the "monstrous wall of water thundering down from above.... I raised my head with open mouth and most of the American cataract went down my throat."

After he dries out, Twain's amazing imagination and sense of fun really takes off. He relates how he stopped to talk to a group of men he takes to be Indians. They turn out to be irate Irishmen who whack him a number of times, tear off his clothes and then pitch him into the river. He goes over the Falls. Eventually pulled out, he's then arrested "for disturbing the peace by yelling at people on shore for help." The judge fines him but Twain has no money since it was in his lost pants. A doctor's examination determines that "only sixteen of my wounds are fatal. I don't mind the others."

So ends a master humorist's account of his Niagara visit.

Spanning Niagara: From Kite to Bridge

24

A kite-flying contest across the Nlagara River in 1848: the beginning of the first suspension bridge. From George W. Holley, *The Falls of Nlagara and Other Famous Cataracts* (1882).

August 1, 1848, is a very significant date in the Niagara story since it was on that day the first bridge across the Niagara Gorge was officially opened.

The chief promoter of the bridge had been William Hamilton Merritt, a Canadian visionary who had also been the driving force behind the building of the first Welland Canal in the 1820s. During the latter part of 1844, Merritt began contacting various businessmen on both sides of the border, asking them if they would support the idea of a suspension bridge at Niagara. While some scoffed at the proposal, those who were interested held a number of organizational meetings. The outcome of these meetings was the formation, in 1846, of two companies, the Niagara Falls Suspension Bridge Company in Canada and the International Bridge Company in New York State. Both companies received a charter from their respective governments that allowed them to jointly construct a carriage bridge "at or near the Falls of Niagara."

Each company was to furnish one half of the money for the construction, maintenance and management of the bridge.

Chosen by the board of directors as chief engineer for the project was Charles Ellet Jr., who had constructed the first suspension bridge in North America across the Schuylkill River, near Philadelphia. He was ecstatic at receiving the Niagara contract since, as he put it, there was no other "single project which would gratify me so much to conduct it to completion." (At the same time, he was also appointed engineer of another suspension bridge that was about to be built across the Ohio River at Wheeling, Virginia, now West Virginia. This bridge still stands.)

Selecting a site for the bridge was easy since at the time it made the most sense to locate it where the gorge was at its narrowest point. This was a spot about 3.2 kilometres (2 miles) below the Falls at the beginning of the Whirlpool Rapids. The bridgehead on the Canadian side would be in what was then a completely undeveloped area (now the foot of Bridge Street), while on the American side there was a small community known as Bellevue, which later became part of the City of Niagara Falls, New York.

Wiliam Hamilton Merritt, the driving force behind the building of the first Welland Canal, was also the chief promoter of the first bridge across the Niagara River.

Francis J. Petrie Collection, Niagara Falls, Ontario, Public Library.

Ellet's first problem was how to establish a link across the gorge. This was solved in January 1848 by holding a kite-flying contest among the young people living on both sides of the border. Just how many entered the competition is not known, but the winner was 15-year-old Homan Walsh of Niagara Falls, New York, who was widely known as an expert in flying kites.

He was brought across the river just below the Falls by ferry, and then walked along the Canadian bank to the site where the bridge was to be constructed. Although it took several tries, Walsh eventually landed his kite on the American side and walked away with five dollars in his pocket. The kite string was then used to pull ropes of increasing size and strength over the gorge until an iron cable could be hauled across.

During the early months of 1848, an ingenious iron basket-chair on rollers was built to run back and forth on the cable. Called Ellet's Basket, it was not only used to carry workmen and supplies from one side of the gorge to the other, but, for a small fee, sightseers could have a ride as well. (Ellet's Basket, which would hold two people, still exists and is now part of the Buffalo and Erie County Historical Society collection.)

By the beginning of July 1848, the bridge was all but finished. It had a length of 228 metres (759 feet). The floor (or deck) was 2.4 metres (eight feet) wide and was suspended from four cables that were anchored over two 17-metre (55-foot) high wooden towers on each bank.

In the *Niagara Mail* for July 12, 1848, the following item appeared: "A friend informs us that the foot path of the Suspension Bridge is finished and that any person can cross it at the expense of a quarter of a dollar. It is said to be of great strength but is in appearance light and flimsy sufficiently so as to deter timid persons or those of weak nerves from venturing on the fancied unsubstantial track. About midway, the view is one of the grandest and most sublime imaginable."

On July 20, Charles Ellet became the first person to drive a horse and carriage across the bridge. He went from the American to the Canadian side and back again while, as it was reported, "being cheered at each end by the spectators."

Twelve days later, the Niagara Suspension Bridge, which quickly became almost as great an attraction as the Falls themselves, was opened to the public. It was successful from the start, but was to have a relatively short life.

In November 1853, the Great Western Railway (now Canadian National) was opened between Hamilton and the Niagara Suspension Bridge. To enable the railway to cross into the United States, work soon began to reconstruct the bridge into a double deck span that would have trains using the upper level while carriages and pedestrians would use the lower floor. The new bridge was completed in March 1855, by which time a small community had evolved at the Canadian end of the span. This Railway Suspension Bridge was used until it was replaced by the present Whirlpool Rapids Bridge at the same site in 1897.

Over the years, these bridges, as well as the railway, have made an enormous contribution to the development of Niagara Falls.

The First Suspension Bridge opened for pedestrian and carriage traffic on August 1, 1848. The view is looking upriver, with the Falls visible in the distance.

Photo of original lithograph. Niagara Falls Heritage Foundation Collection, Niagara Falls, Ontario, Public Library.

The Day the Falls Stopped Flowing

25

A view of the Canadian and American Falls made in the late 1840s. The Falls "ran dry" in March 1848. Pencil sketch, circa 1848. Artist not identified. John Burtniak Collection.

At 5 a.m. on March 29, 1848, Thomas Clark Street was jolted out of a sound sleep by a loud and urgent pounding on his front door.

One of the wealthiest men in the Niagara area, Street lived in a large home known as Clark Hill, which stood on the high bank overlooking what are now known as Dufferin Islands.

He owned an industrial complex consisting mainly of water-powered grist and sawmills that were located below his home beside the rapids of the Niagara River where the now-closed Toronto Powerhouse is today.

When Street reached his front door, he was greeted by his miller who, breathless and excited, told him that the mills had stopped working. Not only was the millrace empty, he reported, but in fact the Niagara River had run dry.

Dumbfounded at such news, Street quickly dressed and ran down the embankment behind his home to the river's edge. There, as he later wrote, "I saw the river channel, on whose banks I had been born 34 years previous, almost entirely dry."

Deciding to wait for more light before investigating any further, Street returned home for some breakfast. He and his sister, who was staying with him at the time, then set out to explore this phenomenon more carefully.

They walked down to Table Rock where an incredible sight met their eyes. The Horseshoe Falls had been reduced to just a trickle of water.

After picking up a long stick, the two walked out along the edge of the virtually waterless Falls, going about a third of the way to Goat Island. Street's sister then tied a handkerchief to the stick and stuck it among some rocks. Her brother stood at the very brink and peered into the gorge below where masses of jagged rocks stood almost completely exposed in the shallow water. He shuddered when he thought about having frequently passed over them on the *Maid of the Mist*. The American Falls was, of course, almost dry as well.

After returning home, Street and his sister took a carriage ride along the Niagara River to Chippawa. During the journey, they noticed some rusty muskets and bayonets lying among the bare rocks on the riverbed. These, they decided, had likely fallen into the river during the early morning hours of July 26, 1814, as the Americans withdrew to their camp at Chippawa following the Battle of Lundy's Lane.

By now, news about the Falls suddenly drying up had spread throughout the area, and many persons had come to witness the amazing spectacle for themselves.

The *Buffalo Express*, in an article featured several days later noted, "All the people in the neighbourhood were abroad, exploring recesses and cavities that had never before been exposed to mortal eyes."

One of the spectators was George Holley of Niagara Falls, New York, who later wrote, "Far up from the head of Goat Island and out into the Canadian Rapids, the water was gone, as it was also from the lower end of Goat Island. The rocks were bare, black and forbidding. The roar of Niagara had subsided to almost a moan." Holley drove a horse and buggy from Goat Island well out onto the riverbed.

The eerily silent spectacle lasted well into the next day, creating excitement that was tinged with apprehension. Then during the evening of March 30, a gathering roar could be heard from the direction of Lake Erie. Like a tidal wave, water came thundering down the Niagara River channel and over the precipice. The familiar and comforting sound of the Falls could be heard once again, and Thomas Clark Street could breathe a sigh of relief as his mills resumed operating.

Niagara residents soon found out the cause of the remarkable incident. The severe winter had created a heavy amount of pack ice in Lake Erie. A strong easterly wind had at first driven this ice up the lake. During the early morning hours of March 29, however, the wind reversed, sending the ice field down the lake, jamming it into the entrance of the Niagara River between Buffalo and Fort Erie. This created a dam that prevented the water from flowing down river.

Only when the wind shifted about 40 hours later did the ice dam break up, releasing the water. So far as is known, nature had never created such a phenomenon at Niagara before, nor has it since.

"A World's Wonder":
Abraham Lincoln Comes to Niagara Falls

26

Barnett's second Niagara Falls Museum, visited by Abraham Lincoln and family in 1857.

Niagara Falls History Museum, Niagara Falls, Ontario.

Among Niagara's visitors during September 1848 was a prominent Springfield, Illinois, lawyer and member of the United States House of Representatives .

His name was Abraham Lincoln. With him was his wife, the former Mary Todd, whom he had married six years before.

Mary had been born in Lexington, Kentucky, and was brought up in a well-to-do, socially prestigious family, a background completely opposite to that of her husband. She met Lincoln in 1839, after having moved to Springfield to live with her older, married sister.

Abraham Lincoln was impressed with Niagara Falls, calling it "a world's wonder." The mighty cascade caused him to ponder philosophically its place in the long sweep of history: "When Columbus first sought this continent – when Christ suffered on the cross – when Moses led Israel through the Red Sea – nay, even, when Adam first came from the hand of his maker – then, as now, Niagara was roaring here."

The Lincolns again came to Niagara Falls in 1857, staying at the Cataract House in Niagara Falls, New York. This famous hotel was destroyed by fire in 1945, but its guest registers were saved and under the date of July 24, 1857, in Lincoln's handwriting, is the entry, "A. Lincoln and family, Springfield, Illinois." Their three sons, Robert, Willie and Tad, were with them on this trip. (A fourth son had died in infancy).

During their stay, a visit was made to the Canadian side of the Niagara River to see, among other things, Thomas Barnett's Niagara Falls Museum. This building was located near the site of the present-day Queen Victoria Place.

In 1860, Abraham Lincoln was elected the 16th President of the United States. Much sorrow, however, awaited him in the White House. Only a month after his inauguration, the American Civil War broke out. Then, in February 1862, William (Willie) died of typhoid fever. He was only 12.

Lincoln won a second term in 1864. It was tragically and violently cut short when he was assassinated by John Wilkes Booth at Washington's Ford Theatre on the evening of April 14, 1865. Mary was beside him that awful night and this shattering shock, combined with Willie's recent death, left her with permanent mental anguish.

As a widow, Mary became obsessed with a fear of poverty (most felt that she had no need for this concern) and worry over her health. She lived in Europe for a time and then, along with her son, Tad, settled in Chicago. Here tragedy again visited Mary Lincoln when 18-year old Tad died of pleurisy on July 15, 1871. Only a few days later, the great Chicago fire broke out and Mary, along with thousands of others, was forced to flee to the Lake Michigan shore while the city burned.

Continued worry about her health brought Mary back to the Niagara area in August 1873. She had decided to visit one of the health spas in St. Catharines that were widely advertised in many parts of the United States at the time. Travelling by steamer to Buffalo, she then boarded a train that took her to Niagara Falls and on to nearby St. Catharines. Here she checked into the fashionable Stephenson House, located on Yates Street, and began taking the baths and drinking the salty, magnesium-laden water.

Mary's mental depression eventually became so acute that Robert, her only surviving son, had her committed to a private sanitarium in 1875. She was released the following year.

Despair, depression and poor health dogged her final years. She travelled some, living in France for a time, and returning to St. Catharines for a few weeks in 1881. Mary died on July 16, 1882, aged 64. She was buried beside her husband in Springfield, the town where she had first met Abraham Lincoln 43 years before.

Mrs. Lincoln visited the Stephenson House, a popular spa hotel in nearby St. Catharines in 1873 and 1881.

From Sheila M. Wilson, *Taking the Waters; A History of the Spas of St. Catharines* (1999).

Isabella Lucy Bird:
An "Englishwoman in America"

27

"As I walked down the slope to the verge of the cliff, I forgot my friends who had called me to the hotel for lunch – I forgot everything – for I was looking at the Falls of Niagara."

These words were written by Isabella Lucy Bird following her first look at Niagara Falls.

An English traveller and author, Isabella came to Niagara in 1854 as part of an extensive tour of eastern North America. Her experiences and observations were recorded in a book she published two years later entitled *The Englishwoman in America.*

Reading her account today gives us some idea of what it was like to experience Niagara in the mid-nineteenth century.

Born in 1832, Isabella was the daughter of a Church of England clergyman. Well educated, she also had the opportunity as a girl to travel a good deal in England and Scotland. These early trips apparently inspired her to make travel writing her vocation.

While visiting Niagara Falls in 1854, world-traveller Isabella Lucy Bird went to the top of Terrapin Tower, which stood almost at the brink of the Horseshoe Falls. She described the sensation as "awful."

From W.H. Withrow, *Our Own Country* (1889).

By the end of the nineteenth century, she had become one of the most popular such writers of her time, having published books about her travels to such places as China, Japan, Hawaii, Korea, Persia and Tibet, as well as North America. Isabella became so successful and respected that in 1893 she became the first woman to be elected as a Fellow of the prestigious Royal Geographical Society.

She was initially disappointed with the Falls, feeling that the human clutter around them took away from their beauty. She noted that on the American side "enormous, many-windowed mills disfigured this romantic spot." The Canadian side wasn't much better, as she wrote, "Even on the British side, where one would have hoped for a better state of things, there is a great fungus growth of museums, curiosity shops, taverns and pagodas with shining tin cupolas."

While at Niagara, Isabella stayed at the Clifton House, which stood at the foot of Clifton Hill. She described this famous hotel as a "huge white block of a building, with three green verandahs around it. It can accommodate about 400 people, and in the summer season it is the abode of almost unparalleled gaiety."

They were met at the entrance of the Clifton House by "about twenty ragged, vociferous carriage drivers, of the most demoralized appearance, all clamorous for a fare." The drivers were continuously insulting and undercutting each other as they competed for business. One of them yelled at Isabella, "I'll take you as cheap as he; he's drunk and his carriage isn't fit for a lady to step into." At that point, a fistfight broke out among a number of the drivers.

In spite of all this turmoil, Isabella and her travelling companions eventually hired a carriage and driver for a sightseeing tour. They were taken along what is now River Road to the Suspension Bridge, which was at the site of the present-day Whirlpool Rapids Bridge. Opened in 1848, the Suspension Bridge was the first span across the Niagara Gorge. At the time of Isabella's visit, it was having a second deck added so that trains could use it.

After paying a toll of 60 cents, they crossed what Isabella called "this extraordinary bridge" and began a tour of the American side. One of the highlights there was a visit to Terrapin Tower which stood almost at the very brink of the Horseshoe Falls. Built in 1833, this 9-metre (30-foot)-high stone observation tower was reached by means of a footbridge from Goat Island. Isabella described the sensation of standing at the top of this tower as "awful."

After visiting a curiosity (souvenir) shop where they "paid for the articles about six times their value," Isabella and her group returned to Canada and were driven to the Whirlpool. She did not like looking at that phenomenon, noting, "The impression which it leaves on the mind is highly unpleasing." Part of this reaction may have come from having been told about the people who had gone over the Falls, whose bodies were later trapped in the Whirlpool.

She then went to Table Rock and had the experience of going "behind the sheet." This popular attraction provided visitors with the opportunity of being guided behind the Horseshoe Falls.

After walking for approximately 60 metres (several hundred feet), you came to what was called Termination Rock, a huge boulder that prevented any further progress. Isabella did not particularly enjoy this excursion and wrote, "The front view is the only one for Niagara. Going behind the sheet is like going behind a picture frame."

Following many hours of frantic activity, Isabella now wanted some quiet time to be alone with the Falls so she could come to know them on her own terms. Accordingly, she climbed down to the ferry landing and made her way out to the furthest rock in the river that she could safely reach. Here she remained for nearly four hours, reflecting on the scene before her. As she wrote, "I sat down completely undisturbed in view of the mighty falls. I was not distracted by parasitic guides or sandwich-eating visitors; the vile museums, pagodas and tea-gardens were out of sight."

Night had fallen before she returned to the Clifton House. She now felt that the "sublimity of the Falls far exceeded my expectations, and I appreciated them more perhaps from having been disappointed with the first view."

One of the 19th century's best-known travel writers, Isabella Lucy Bird died in 1904.

"Splendour and Brilliancy": Samuel Zimmerman Throws a Party

28

It must have been some party! In fact, a reporter for the Toronto *Daily Leader* was so awed he wrote that it was "one of the largest and most brilliant assemblies ever convened in Canada."

This great gathering had been held in Niagara Falls on Wednesday, October 31, 1855, at the Clifton House Hotel (now the site of Oakes Garden Theatre). The host was Samuel Zimmerman, who also happened to own the Clifton House.

An invitation to Mr. Zimmerman's Ball, October 31, 1855.
Niagara Falls History Museum, Niagara Falls, Ontario.

Zimmerman had come to Canada from Pennsylvania in 1842. After making a considerable amount of money through Welland Canal reconstruction contracts, he turned his attention to railway building, including the Great Western (now Canadian National) line between Hamilton and Niagara, which was completed in 1853.

In 1848 Zimmerman married Mary Ann Woodruff of St. Davids. In the years that followed, he began laying out a large estate on land that overlooked the American Falls, including what is now the northern portion of Queen Victoria Park. He also bought up a great deal of other property in the area, including the Clifton House.

One of the chief reasons for Zimmerman's great success was his ability as a political lobbyist, especially in railway matters. The individual he became closest to in government circles was Francis Hincks. During the early 1850s Hincks was Canada's Premier and Finance Minister. As such, he was the most influential member of the Board of Railway Commissioners which had been formed to screen all applications to the legislature for railway charters. When Hinck's government was defeated in 1854 Zimmerman lost a powerful and sympathetic political ally.

The following year the British government appointed Francis Hincks Governor of Barbados. As a send-off and tribute to his friend, Samuel Zimmerman decided to throw one of the biggest parties Niagara had ever seen.

While both men and women were invited, the evening began with a huge banquet for the men only. Included among the 300 guests were Allan MacNab, Premier of pre-Confederation Canada at the time, and a host of cabinet members, including John A. Macdonald, who would become Canada's first Prime Minister in 1867. The menu for this dinner was little short of incredible. To begin, there were two soups and fish dishes, along with boiled ham, mutton and turkey, each with its own sauce. Next came roasts of ham, turkey, beef and lamb. Seven cold and ornamental dishes were available, followed by 11 different entrees. After this came the game and vegetable dishes, including venison, canvasback ducks, prairie chicken, three types of potatoes, onions, turnips, beets, and squash. To cap off the

On October 31, 1855 Samuel Zimmerman hosted one of the most sumptuous parties ever to be held at the Clifton House Hotel.

Kiwanis Club of Stamford, Ontario, Inc., *Niagara Falls, Canada; A History of the City* (1967).

meal, there as a choice of such items as plum or rice pudding, apple pie, orange pie, quince tarts, wine jelly, lemon ice cream, grapes, walnuts, almonds and raisins.

Many speeches and toasts followed the dinner. The men then joined the ladies to view a spectacular fireworks display set off from Zimmerman's property on the other side of Clifton Hill.

By now it was nearly 11 o'clock and everyone headed to the ballroom for dancing. An eyewitness to much of the evening, although not an invited guest, was 19-year-old Sidney Barnett, whose father, Thomas, owned the Niagara Falls Museum, then located near Table Rock. Sidney wrote in his diary how he went up to the gallery above the Clifton House ballroom to watch the grand affair. He estimated that there were at least 600 people on the floor below. Very impressed, he wrote, "Such a splendour of dress I never saw before. Each one tried to outdo the other. There were very many pretty ladies there.... I did not stay a great while for the splendour and brilliancy of the scene was bedizening."

At 1:30 a.m. a supper was served. The Toronto reporter noted: "The table groaned with a sumptuous fare, which wines of renowned vintage made more attractive. The entire Clifton House for eating, drinking, smoking and talking was thrown open to the guests."

The party finally broke up around 4:00 a.m., mainly because many of the guests had to get down to the Bridge Street railway station in order to catch the five o'clock train for Toronto.

Among these was the *Daily Leader* reporter who, apparently still dazzled by what he had seen, later wrote, "A display like that which took place at the Clifton House on Wednesday evening is of so rare occurrence that we cannot at this moment recall anything similar in the history of public demonstrations."

Blondin:
Artistry on a Rope

29

This photograph is one of the most famous and dramatic ever taken at Niagara Falls. Blondin, the world's foremost tightrope walker, is seen carrying his manager, Harry Colcord, across the Niagara Gorge on his back.

Niagara Parks Archives.

It was June 30, 1859. Thousands of people were gathered along both sides of the Niagara River Gorge that summer afternoon. They were witnessing an unbelievable sight – a man performing stunts with incredible skill and daring on a 5-centimetre (2-inch)-thick rope that was stretched across the river, high above the racing water. The performer was Jean Francois Gravelet, much better known by his stage name of Blondin.

Born in St. Omer, France, in 1824, Jean began demonstrating an extraordinary talent in gymnastics by the age of four. Recognizing his son's ability, his father enrolled him in a school of gymnastics where he soon became known as 'The Little Wonder'. By the time he left the school four years later, he could not only walk on the tightrope with great skill, but could dance on it and do somersaults.

For about the next 20 years, he performed all over France, perfecting his skills and adding to his repertoire of stunts. It was during this time he adopted the stage name of 'Blondin', owing to his fair hair and skin.

In the early 1850s, Blondin was invited to join Gabriel Ravel's famous circus troupe and quickly became one of its major stars as the circus toured many parts of Europe. Ravel later brought his show to the United States and in 1858, while appearing in Buffalo, New York, Blondin visited Niagara Falls as a tourist. He was immediately seized with the idea of doing something never before attempted – crossing the Niagara River Gorge on a tightrope. As he later wrote, "To cross those roaring waters became the ambition of my life."

And so it was that on Thursday, June 30, 1859, after months of careful preparation and considerable publicity, all was in readiness. A crowd estimated at 10,000 (many of whom were paying customers in special grandstands) was on hand to watch Blondin's first performance at Niagara Falls. His rope spanned the gorge approximately 1.6 kilometres (one mile) below the Falls, about midway between today's Rainbow and Whirlpool Rapids Bridges.

The show began at 4:45 p.m., with Blondin starting out from the American side. The moment of truth had arrived. Would his years of experience be enough to meet this challenge, or would he find injury or death in the tumultuous waters nearly 60 metres (200 feet) below?

With his 22.5 kilogram (50-pound) balancing pole in hand, Blondin marched on at a lively pace, "his toes hardly appearing to touch the rope," as one newspaper reporter wrote. About a third of the way out, he sat down on the rope and, following a prearranged plan, waved his arm for the *Maid of the Mist* steamboat to come up beneath him. After it was in position, Blondin lay on the rope and lowered a length of cord to the little boat's deck. The men on board the steamer then tied a bottle of wine to the cord. After Blondin pulled up the bottle, he stood on his rope, held the bottle over his head for all the spectators to see, drank the contents, tossed the empty bottle over his shoulder into the river and then continued his perilous journey.

After a performance time of about 20 minutes, Blondin reached the Canadian side. He was clearly tired, but was also smiling and very happy. The crowd went wild. After an hour's rest, during which he drank some champagne and changed his clothes, he was ready for the return trip on the rope. This he accomplished in eight minutes, running most of the way.

Blondin gave another seven tightrope performances at Niagara Falls that summer. Some of his other stunts included crossing blindfolded, walking backwards, standing on his head, crossing while his ankles and wrists were shackled, hanging from the rope by his hands and then his feet, turning somersaults and making a nighttime trip with flares on the ends of his balancing pole to light the way.

On one occasion, he carried out a 22.5-kilogram (55-pound) stove, stopped near the centre of the rope and cooked several omelets. These were then lowered in a pan to passengers on the *Maid of the Mist* directly below.

His most famous stunt, however, came on August 17, when he carried his manager, Harry Colcord, across on his back. Colcord was not a ropewalker, although Blondin had previously carried him on his back during a number of indoor shows.

UNPARALLELLED
TIGHT-ROPE
ASCENSION,
BY THE INTREPID
BLONDIN,
AT NIAGARA FALLS,
—: ON :—
Wednesday, June 20.

ON THIS OCCASION MONS. BLONDIN will execute one of the most daring feats ever performed by man— that of

Walking the Entire Length of his Rope,

Which is 1,000 feet, and 200 feet above the boiling hell of Niagara River,

BLINDFOLDED, AND TIED UP IN A SACK

From head to foot. Mons. Blondin will also

STAND ON HIS HEAD

when in the centre of his rope, and directly over the fearful rapids.

☞ Photographs of Mons. Blondin, by O. B. Evans of Buffalo, N. Y., for sale at all the principal Hotels at Niagara Falls, for 25 cts. each.

June 16, 1860]   HARRY COLCORD Agent.

A broadside advertising one of Blondin's performances at Niagara Falls.

Niagara Falls Heritage Foundation, Niagara Falls, Ontario, Public Library.

Nevertheless, this performance over the Niagara River turned out to be a supreme challenge for both men. Colcord had to dismount and stand on the rope seven times while Blondin rested. Finally, after 45 tense minutes, the two men safely reached the other side of the gorge. For Blondin, this had been his greatest achievement.

Blondin's exploits at Niagara Falls had created a sensation, giving him international celebrity status. Capitalizing on this fame, he triumphantly toured Europe during the winter of 1859-60. The following summer, he was back at Niagara Falls for another series of amazing performances. This time, his rope was stretched across the river just north of where the Whirlpool Rapids Bridge is now.

One of his new stunts that year was to cross while wearing stilts. He also carried Harry Colcord across again – twice. The second time was during a very special performance given in honour of the Prince of Wales' visit to Niagara Falls. (He later became King Edward VII). The date was September 15, 1860, and a throng estimated at 100,000 was on hand to see both the Prince and what was Blondin's farewell performance at Niagara Falls. He continued to perform, never with a mishap, all over the world until 1896, when ill health forced him to retire to his English estate, which he had named 'Niagara.' It was there that he died in his bed on February 22, 1897, six days before his 73rd birthday.

One of the greatest tightrope artists of all time, Blondin gave some of his most brilliant and memorable performances at Niagara Falls. In so doing, his name and Niagara's became inseparably linked.

Going Behind the Sheet of Water | 30

J.C. Bonnefons obviously had more than the usual amount of courage and curiosity.

This was amply demonstrated during April 1753, when he and two friends visited Niagara Falls. After viewing the cataract from Table Rock, Bonnefons proposed that they climb down the side of the gorge to the foot of the waterfall. His friends were horrified at such an idea. Since there was no path of any kind, it would mean clinging to bushes and roots while using small rock ledges for toeholds as you lowered yourself into the gorge. One false step and you would be hurled into eternity.

His fellow travelers refused to take part in such a risky venture, so Bonnefons, undaunted, undertook the perilous descent on his own. He soon realized that he had taken on more than he had bargained for but as he later wrote: "I had to finish as much from pride as from curiosity." An hour later he had reached the bottom of the gorge.

In this 1889 sketch, a group of intrepid tourists is seen passing behind the "Great Falling Sheet of Water" – the Horseshoe Falls. From W.H. Withrow, *Our Own Country* (1889).

Drenched by spray, Bonnefons clamored over the slippery rocks to the base of the cataract. His adventuresome spirit then propelled him to see if it was possible to go behind the Falls. It was. Although the overwhelming roar, combined with the trembling of the rocks was both deafening and disconcerting, he cautiously moved in behind the vast curtain of crashing water.

There, he found a wide cavern around 6 metres (20 feet) high and 4.5 metres (15 feet) deep. Large clefts in the rock prevented any further progress, forcing Bonnefons to retreat.

When he finally got back to his friends on top of the gorge, he was soaked, cold and temporarily deaf. It was several hours before his hearing returned. Bonnefons' account is one of the earliest descriptions in existence of a "trip" behind the Horseshoe Falls.

In 1818, local entrepreneur William Forsyth built a spiral stairway down the side of the gorge near Table Rock. With access now much easier and safer, many more people, women as well as men, began to make the descent into the gorge and explore the area behind the Falls.

By 1827, a "Trip Behind the Great Falling Sheet of Water" as it was named, had become a relatively popular and organized attraction. Captain Basil Hall visited Niagara Falls during June 1827, and wrote how on three occasions he visited "the extraordinary cave formed between the cascade and the face of the overhanging cliff." He was conducted each time by an experienced guide who made a "handsome livelihood" leading these tours.

Hall reported that it was possible to walk some distance behind the Falls before a huge piece of limestone, which came to be known as Termination Rock, blocked the way.

In the autumn of 1827, the wealthy partnership of Thomas Clark and Samuel Street bought out Forsyth's stairway and cave attraction. They immediately sublet the business to W.D. Wright.

Around the same time, Clark and Street constructed two small buildings at Table Rock. One had dressing rooms where visitors could don their waterproof clothing for the "Trip Behind the Falling Sheet of Water to Termination Rock." The other was built at the top of the stairway and housed a barroom.

W.D. Wright came up with the idea of offering (for a fee) a signed certificate to each person who had successfully reached Termination Rock. It would be a souvenir of your visit and a reminder of your accomplishment.

This practice was continued by Isaiah Starkey, who became keeper of the stairway at Table Rock in 1834. He held the job for 11 years and was a familiar figure around Niagara Falls.

Starkey permitted free access to the stairway, but in order to reach the stairs one had to pass through his barroom. Here, he not only sold liquor, but ice cream, lemonade and pastries as well. As might be expected, Starkey also charged a fee for both the waterproof clothing and guide service.

In addition, the barroom housed a display of various minerals and tables holding guest registers. (Starkey had a celebrity guest in 1842 when Charles Dickens dropped by.)

A number of 19th century visitors to Niagara Falls wrote about their experience behind the Horseshoe Falls. Most commented on the ear-splitting noise, getting soaked (in spite of wearing what was supposed to be waterproof clothing) and being buffeted by the strong wind currents.

John Fowler added another interesting detail. He made the trip in 1830 and noted in his journal how the walking was made more difficult "by the number of small eels which are twisting about under your feet in all directions."

Nevertheless, the majority of people felt that it was an exhilarating, unique and memorable experience.

The modern-day version of going Behind the Great Falling Sheet of Water is the Journey Behind the Falls, operated by The Niagara Parks Commission. Located at Table Rock and operated year-round, visitors descend 37.5 metres (125 feet) through the gorge wall by elevator. A short tunnel then provides access to two outdoor observation decks and two portals directly behind the Falls.

Having this experience helps people to realize just how accurate J.C. Bonnefons was back in 1753, when he described Niagara Falls as an "astonishing cataract."

Joel Robinson: Through the Whirlpool Rapids on the *Maid of the Mist*

31

The *Maid of the Mist*, making its perilous journey through the Whirlpool Rapids, in June 1861. From Kiwanis Club of Stamford, Ontario, Inc., *Niagara Falls, Canada; A History of the City* (1967).

During the mid-1800s, one of the best-known individuals along both sides of the Niagara River was Joel Robinson.

His fame developed as the result of a number of dramatic rescues he had made of people who had got into trouble in the river, particularly around the area of the Falls. Robinson and his small red skiff became so adept at successfully carrying out these rescue operations that he became known as the Navigator of the Rapids.

He was born in Springfield, Massachusetts, and came to Niagara Falls, New York, as a young man. Nearly 1.8 metres (6 feet) tall, with light chestnut hair, blue eyes and a fair complexion, Robinson was described by a writer of the day as "cool, deliberate, lithe and kindhearted." Obviously courageous as well, he was very much at home in or on the water and had a considerable knowledge of the Niagara River.

All of these qualities made him a natural choice to be selected as captain for the second *Maid of the Mist*, which was launched on July 14, 1854, at its United States dock. (The first *Maid* had served from 1846 until replaced by this successor.) It was a single-stack, steam-driven, paddle wheel vessel a little over 22 metres (72 feet) in length.

Due to the owner's financial difficulties, the *Maid of the Mist* was sold following the close of the 1860 tourist season. A Montreal firm purchased the craft on the condition that it be delivered to Lake Ontario. This meant attempting something that had never been done before – taking a boat through the Lower Rapids and Whirlpool of the Niagara River, one of the most dangerous stretches of white water in the world. In addition, it is important to remember that in those days considerably more water flowed through this section of the river since there were no diversions for electrical generation being made as we now have.

Robinson, it was noted at the time, had a "strange, almost irrepressible desire" to pilot the *Maid* on the extremely perilous trip through the rapids. He was offered $500 to make the journey. Engineer James Jones and fireman James McIntyre also agreed to go along for $100 each.

In the early afternoon of June 6, 1861, Robinson wheeled the *Maid* away front her dock on the New York side of the river, just above the present Whirlpool Rapids Bridge. He first steamed towards the Falls, then swung her around and headed downstream until she was caught in the rapids. The little boat was battered and slashed with incredible fury. The first big wave to strike the *Maid* heeled her over, snapped off the funnel and threw Robinson flat on his back. She soon righted herself, however, and charged on downriver.

McIntyre was later interviewed about the historic trip by the *New York Tribune* and gave a graphic account of what it was like. He said, in part, "I had no fear at the start, but after we got into those Rapids I would have given worlds to get ashore. The Rapids themselves are a mile in length and two minutes was the time of the passage. That is pretty fast travelling through a current 60 feet higher in mid-stream than at the sides in an unnavigated channel. Every moment was one of expected death. We were tossed about in the hold, Jones and I, until it seemed that the quick succession of shocks would kill us."

Luckily, the boat was able to avoid getting trapped in the Whirlpool. McIntyre explained how this happened: "At the entrance to it the *Maid's* stern grounded lightly on a rock. She swung around and shot downstream instead of following the current into the Whirlpool."

Robinson successfully brought the bruised but triumphant *Maid* up to the Queenston dock. The whole trip had taken about 16 minutes. It was, apparently, a day for a miracle. Nevertheless, he still had to make out a customs form and pay a port fee.

It sometimes happens that those who have attempted feats close to the impossible then lose their desire for defiance. Joel Robinson, according to his wife, "was 20 years older when he came home that day than when he went out." A local contemporary writer, George Holley, noted, "Both his manner and appearance were changed. Calm and deliberate before, he became thoughtful and serious afterward. He had been borne, as it were, in the arms of a power so mighty that its impress was stamped on his features and on his mind. Through a slightly opened door he had seen a vision which awed and subdued him. He became reverent in a moment. He grew venerable in an hour."

Gilbert McMicken: Undercover Agent and Mayor

32

On October 19, 1864, during the American Civil War, the little town of St. Albans, Vermont, was the scene of a remarkable incident. On that day, about 20 Confederate soldiers, who had travelled south from Quebec and quietly congregated in the community over the preceding few weeks, suddenly announced that they were taking over the town. The residents were herded onto the village green and kept under guard by several of the Southerners, while their compatriots robbed the banks, set several buildings on fire and generally shot up the place. They then mounted stolen horses and headed back to the Canadian border.

Led by a Union Army Captain, a posse was quickly formed which pursued the Confederates right into Quebec, where British troops then took the Southerners into custody.

Gilbert McMicken had a full and varied career.
Library and Archives Canada, Ottawa.

The St. Alban's Raid focused attention in the northern United States on Confederate activities in Canada. These were greatly resented, not to mention illegal under British neutrality laws. Canada was properly embarrassed and promptly stationed 2,000 militia along the border to prevent any further such actions.

At the same time, John A. Macdonald, Attorney-General for Canada West (Ontario), decided to form an undercover police force, partly to gather more information on both Confederate and Union activities taking place in Canada. To head this new organization, Macdonald chose Gilbert McMicken, a man well-known in the Niagara area. He had, in fact, been the first Mayor of Clifton, now part of the City of Niagara Falls.

McMicken followed a number of career paths during his lifetime. Born in London, England, in 1813, he grew up in Scotland. In 1832 he immigrated to Canada and settled in Chippawa, where he opened a forwarding business. On February 19, 1835, he married Ann Teresa Duff of Chippawa. In the years that followed, they had six children and adopted a seventh.

Two years later the McMickens moved to Queenston where Gilbert became Collector of Customs.

He entered banking for a time and then, during the 1840s, leased and managed the 16-kilometre (10-mile) long, horse-drawn Erie and Ontario Railroad between Queenston and Chippawa. (Much of its route followed the line of what is now Stanley Avenue in Niagara Falls.)

Real estate and insurance next attracted his attention, while at the same time politics became a passion. In 1851 he became Warden of the United Counties of Lincoln and Welland.

Later that same year, he moved to Clifton. Here McMicken continued to be involved in a variety of interests and government positions. When Clifton was incorporated in 1856, he became its first mayor and also took on the posts of school board chairman and postmaster. He was one of the driving forces in organizing the Presbyterian congregation in Clifton. During this time he built a large home for his family on what is now Victoria Avenue. The house, considerably altered, still stands and may be seen just behind the Bell Canada building.

It was during these years that he became well acquainted with John A. Macdonald, who later became Canada's first Prime Minister in 1867. At the time of McMicken's appointment as head of the new Canadian undercover police force, Macdonald described him as a "shrewd, cool and determined man who won't easily lose his head, and who will fearlessly perform his duty."

These qualities undoubtedly ensured McMicken's success with the job and also secured for him a variety of other government positions over the years. For example, in 1869 he was appointed Commissioner of the new Dominion Police, a force organized to protect federal buildings in Ottawa. Following the creation of the Province of Manitoba in 1870, he was sent to Winnipeg to establish a number of federal government offices in the new provincial capital.

He later moved there permanently and in 1879 was elected to the Legislative Assembly of Manitoba.

Gilbert McMicken died in Winnipeg on March 7, 1891.

When the news of his passing reached Niagara, no doubt many older residents recalled the energetic community builder who had played such an important role in the very early years of Niagara Falls.

The home of Gilbert McMicken, 1856, on Victoria Avenue, Niagara Falls.
From Kiwanis Club of Stamford, Ontario, Inc., *Niagara Falls, Canada; A History of the City* (1967).

90

Confederates at Niagara Falls: Intrigue During the American Civil War

33

It was a cataclysmic event of enormous and tragic numbers. The U.S. Civil War (1861-1865) saw more than three million Americans under arms, some 600,000 of whom died. Although Canada remained neutral, many thousands of Canadians fought in the war as volunteers, with around 5,000 dying in the epic struggle. Some of these young men came from what is now Niagara Falls.

A group of Confederate agents pose for the camera in what is now Queen Victoria Park during the summer of 1864. The American Falls may be seen in the background. Standing at the left is George Sanders who met with Horace Greeley here that year after Greeley came from New York to investigate the possibility of starting talks to end the Civil War.

Sherman Zavitz Collection.

Niagara also played an interesting role in the war, especially during the latter years of the conflict, when it became one of several centers of operation for Confederate agents.

Well-financed, Confederate activities in Canada focused on an elaborate plan referred to as the Northwest Conspiracy. Using a variety of means, the ultimate aim of this conspiracy was the overthrow of Abraham Lincoln and his government. Beginning in 1864, as the South's fortunes waned, agents of the Confederate States held a number of clandestine meetings, some of which were in Niagara Falls, to organize a variety of violent and disruptive actions in the North, all designed to create trouble for Lincoln. These included the capture of two American ships on Lake Erie, freeing prisoners-of-war, burning down hotels in New York City and even kidnapping the vice president. However, none of these escapades across the border into Union territory was an unqualified success.

One of the local businesses used by Confederate agents was Thomas Barnett's Niagara Falls Museum, which was located at the foot of Murray Hill where Queen Victoria Place is now. A courier or visiting agent would enter the museum and sign the guest register, thus announcing his presence to locally based agents who regularly inspected the register. Messages could then be exchanged or meetings organized according to prearranged plans. Local agents could meet the visitor among crowds of tourists where they would not be easily noticed. At the same time, the visitor wouldn't know where the Niagara agents actually lived.

However, the most intriguing episode to take place at Niagara Falls during the Civil War involved the famed editor of the *New York Tribune*, Horace Greeley. This was a powerful partnership since the *Tribune* was the most influential newspaper in the United States and Greeley was a close friend of President Lincoln.

By early 1864, Greeley was privately urging Lincoln to seek a negotiated settlement with the South to end the bloody war. Then one of Greeley's wealthy and eccentric friends, William Jewett, suddenly entered the picture. On July 5, 1864, Jewett sent a letter to Greeley from Niagara Falls indicating that two "ambassadors" of the Confederacy "with full and complete powers for a peace" were in Niagara. He urged Greeley to use his influence with Lincoln to act on the matter.

Although Jewett had the reputation in some circles as a "meddlesome blockhead" and a "crack-brained simpleton," Greeley was excited by the news and notified Jewett he would get involved. He then sent Jewett's letter and one of his own to Lincoln, pleading with the president to offer safe conduct to the two men so they could come to Washington and discuss peace.

Lincoln responded that he would meet with them provided they had a signed statement from Jefferson Davis, president of the Confederacy, which agreed to the restoration of the union and the end of slavery. Greeley knew the South would never agree to these preconditions but not wanting to jeopardize any possible peace talks, decided not to mention the president's terms to the Confederates until later.

After a flurry of correspondence between Washington and New York, Greeley was deputized to go to Niagara Falls and meet the alleged peace emissaries of Jefferson Davis. Lincoln's personal secretary, John Hay, was to accompany him.

So it was that on July 20, 1864, Greeley and Hay walked into the barroom of the Clifton House Hotel. Niagara Falls' largest and most glamorous hotel, the Clifton House stood on the site now occupied by Oakes Garden Theatre.

Many of the hotel's guests immediately recognized Greeley so that, as Hay later wrote, "The barroom began to fill and the hall outside to bloom with wide-eyed and pretty women."

At the Clifton House, Greeley met with George Sanders and James Holcombe, both Confederate agents. To his great chagrin, however the *Tribune's* editor soon learned that, despite William Jewett's claim, these men were not accredited by Jefferson Davis and would not go to Washington on the terms demanded by Lincoln.

Disappointed and frustrated, Greeley returned home, his Niagara Falls peace initiative having quickly collapsed.

Burr Plato: The Underground Railroad to the Promised Land

34

The Underground Railroad had no tracks or timetables but it did have conductors, stations and many passengers.

From around 1830 to 1860, some 50,000 slaves from the southern United States used this "railroad" to reach freedom in Canada – the promised land.

It was 'underground' in that it was a secret mission run by courageous individuals willing to help guide and transport escaped slaves. The 'conductors' drove carts or wagons with secret compartments, while the 'stations' were a variety of places, such as barns and belfries, that were used for hiding the fugitives during the day, since travelling was mostly done at night.

A scroll of appreciation presented to Burr Plato's widow and family in 1905 expressing the high regard in which he was held by the citizens of the City of Niagara Falls.

The Norval Johnson Heritage Library, Niagara Falls, Ontario.

There were a number of routes, some of which ended at Black Rock (Buffalo), Lewiston and Youngstown on the east bank of the Niagara River. Ferry captains at these 'terminals' were usually sympathetic and would not charge for the trip across the river. Beginning in 1855, some fugitives entered Canada by train at Niagara Falls, using the new Railway Suspension Bridge, which was located where the Whirlpool Rapids Bridge is today.

Black settlements, comprised of former slaves, developed in various areas of southern Ontario. One of these was at Drummondville, as the community centred around the Main and Ferry intersection of present-day Niagara Falls, Ontario, was called.

Occasionally there were attempts to kidnap local blacks and take them back to the United States. One such incident occurred during the 1850s when the manager of the famous Clifton House Hotel (which stood where Oakes Garden Theatre is now situated) collaborated with American kidnappers to capture Sarah Giddings, who worked at the hotel, and return her to slavery. A group of her friends found out about the plot and got her to safety, foiling the scheme.

One of the most renowned blacks in Niagara Falls was Burr Plato. He was born into slavery in Virginia. Over the years he managed to save $50 and in 1856, at the age of 22, he and seven other blacks fled the state for Canada. Using the Underground Railroad, they reached Black Rock where, not trusting the ferry, they jumped into the Niagara River and swam across to Fort Erie, arriving on Canadian soil with only five dollars and a bag of biscuits among them.

Determined to succeed, Plato first worked as a farmhand in Stamford Township, now part of Niagara Falls. Later, he was a porter during the day and tended limekilns in the evening. He also took classes to learn to read and write.

By 1870, after having saved enough money to purchase horses and a carriage, he had become a hackman, providing the same services that local tour and taxi operators do today.

At the time, hackmen in the Niagara area had a notorious reputation as swindlers. Plato, however, was known as "the only honest hackman around Niagara Falls." His business was very successful, allowing him to buy a home on Stanley Avenue.

Here he and his wife, Mary, lived and raised their ten children. It became one of the first houses in Niagara Falls to have gas lighting. During the following years, he bought a considerable amount of property around the area.

He was also a strong supporter and member of the British Methodist Episcopal Church, which still stands on Peer Street.

Popular and respected, Plato was nominated and then elected as a councilor for the Village of Niagara Falls (formerly Drummondville) in January 1886. This was quite an achievement since during the nineteenth century only a handful of blacks were elected to public office in Canada. He was re-elected as a councilor almost every year until 1901.

Burr Plato died on September 27, 1905, and was buried in Drummond Hill Cemetery. The flag at city hall on Queen Street, in what was by then the City of Niagara Falls, was lowered to half-mast as a mark of respect. A tribute in the local press noted: "There are few men who can claim more real credit at the end of their life's work than Burr Plato."

Lord Dufferin:
A Public Park for Niagara

35

One of the most influential visitors Niagara Falls has ever had was Lord Dufferin, Governor-General of Canada from 1872 to 1878.

He and his wife, Lady Dufferin, made their first visit here for a week, beginning on Monday, September 30, 1872. Lady Dufferin wrote that she was "not in the least disappointed with the falls."

She also described their visit to the Cave of the Winds on the American side: "I was surprised to find we

Cartoonist Duncan Macpherson's interpretation of the notorious "Front" (the area around the Horseshoe Falls) in pre-Niagara Park Commission days.

From Kiwanis Club of Stamford, Ontario, Inc., *Niagara Falls, Canada: A History of the City* (1967).

were expected to array ourselves in yellow oil-cloth trousers, with jackets and hoods of the same material. We climbed over rocks and small wooden bridges until we came to the Falls, and walked behind it, in a complete shower-bath, but I enjoyed it immensely. We did look a funny yellow party, dripping with water."

The Governor-General and his wife came again in late August 1874. Lady Dufferin wrote that, having seen many waterfalls, as far as Niagara was concerned, "None approach it. We saw it in beautiful sunshine, with a perfect rainbow joining the Falls."

While obviously impressed with the cataracts themselves, Lord and Lady Dufferin were not nearly so pleased with what they saw going on in the vicinity of the Falls.

The entire area around the Horseshoe Falls on the Canadian side was commonly called the "Front," and was the breeding ground of some of the worst con artists on the continent. Visitors were regularly swindled, blackmailed and bullied.

American author Henry James came to Niagara one year before Lord and Lady Dufferin's first visit and described the following scene: "The spectacle you have come so far to see is choked with horribly vulgar shops, booths and catch-penny artifices which have pushed and elbowed to within the very spray of the Falls. The inopportunities one suffers here amid the central din of the cataract from hackmen, photographers and vendors of gimmicks is simply hideous and infamous."

One of the most notorious businesses was Table Rock House, owned for many years by Saul Davis. The Hamilton *Evening Times* once described this place as "the den of forty thieves." Davis' employees sweetly invited visitors into his establishment and encouraged them to take a trip to the base of the Horseshoe Falls, all for free. When they tried to leave, however, it was a different story. One tourist reported that he was ordered to pay four dollars before he would be let out the door. He refused. At that point he was grabbed by the throat, pushed out the door and knocked to the ground. In some ways he was lucky. Many others were threatened and robbed before being thrown out.

By the 1870s it was clear to many that this blight on Niagara's beauty had to go. Lord Dufferin was one of these and during a speech before the Ontario Society of Artists at Toronto in 1878, he made the first public suggestion that the area around the Falls should be turned into a public park. He followed this up with a letter urging the Ontario Government to take an interest in the concept.

Despite strong representation to establish a park at Niagara, the Canadian federal government took no action. Prime Minister Sir John A. Macdonald apparently feared that national parks would be requested in many places if one were established at Niagara.

Consequently, it was left to the Province of Ontario to take the lead. In 1885 it passed the 'Niagara Falls Park Act.' Over the next several years all the private property along the "Front" was expropriated, and in 1888 the 62-hectare (154-acre) Queen Victoria Park was opened to the public.

While Lord and Lady Dufferin were no longer in Canada, they were undoubtedly pleased to hear that the idea of creating a park at Niagara had been acted upon. Ontario, to recognize the role Dufferin had played in the project, named the group of islands just above the Horseshoe Falls in his honour.

This 1885 view shows the carriage and pedestrian bridge leading to what are now known as Dufferin Islands, just above the Horseshoe Falls. Lord Dufferin, Canada's third Governor-General, promoted the idea of establishing a public park in the area around the Falls.

From *Tugby's Illustrated Guide to Niagara Falls* (1885). Sherman Zavitz Collection.

The "Grand Buffalo Hunt": Wild Bill Hickok at Niagara

36

During August of 1872, posters began appearing in the Niagara area advertising what was described as a 'Grand Buffalo Hunt' that was to take place in Niagara Falls, Ontario, on the 28th and 30th of the month.

The publicity went on to say, "This novel and most exciting affair will be under the direction and management of the most celebrated scout and hunter of the great plains, Mr. William Hickok, better known as Wild Bill."

Thomas Barnett, who owned the Niagara Falls Museum, was sponsoring the elaborate show.

Barnett, a native of England, had founded his museum in 1827 in a small stone building at the foot of Murray Hill, near the Horseshoe Falls. An expansion came ten years later. In 1858, he moved this building slightly to the south and converted it into a hotel. Then on the former museum site, where Queen Victoria Place now stands, he built a large cut stone building that cost around $140,000.

It was filled with thousands of items, including many stuffed animals, since both Thomas and his son, Sidney, were expert taxidermists.

Barnett was known as a reputable business-man and his museum became a extremely popular attraction. He also was a great Niagara promoter, with the buffalo hunt being his most ambitious undertaking.

It had taken over a year of work, which had included a number of frustrations and delays, to organize what was billed as a "thrilling spectacle." Sidney had made two trips to Nebraska to hire Indians, buy the buffalo and take care of all the other necessary

A poster announcing the "Grand Buffalo Hunt," held in August 1872, with the famed "Wild Bill" Hickok in charge.

Niagara Falls History Museum, Niagara Falls, Ontario.

arrangements. He even managed to sign up "Wild Bill" Hickok to direct the event.

The 'Grand Buffalo Hunt' was staged on a 6-hectare (15-acre) site at Fallsview, an area on the highbank, just above the Falls. The grounds had at one time been used for a racetrack.

A board fence about 2.5 metres (8 feet) high enclosed the whole area. Around 2,000 spectators, who were charged an admission fee of 50 cents per person, were accommodated on tiers of seats at the northeast end of the compound. It was a disappointing crowd for Barnett, however, who needed many more people in the stands just to break even.

The show got under way at 3 p.m. with a lacrosse match featuring Native Canadians from the Grand River area of Southern Ontario.

Then a group of mounted 'hunters' appeared. They included "Wild Bill" Hickok, four Native Americans, and an equal number of Mexicans who were wearing large sombreros, black velvet jackets and yellow pants. They all rode up to a pen in the centre of the enclosure where two buffalo and a Texas ox were standing.

A reporter covering the event for the local press noted: "The first game struck was a Texas ox, but he was not taking a lively interest in the affair and was soon turned out to grass."

A buffalo cow was then brought out but didn't seem to understand that she was to provide a "thrilling spectacle." Consequently, as the reporter commented, she "loafed around and then laid down." Finally persuaded to stand up, she was lassoed and pulled back into the pen.

Next, a "rather rangy looking" buffalo, a bull, came out from the pen "as leisurely as a deacon from church."

The animal was eventually prodded enough to make it run while the Native Americans gave chase, but it ran so slowly that they often passed it. After half an hour's "fooling around like this," the bull became winded and stopped to graze.

The show was over.

While undoubtedly some people enjoyed the program, many did not and felt, like the reporter, that it had been a "swindle" and a "farce."

Thomas Barnett lost heavily on the event and five years later, after continuing financial reverses, was forced to sell his beloved museum. He died at the age of 91 in 1890, and was buried in Drummond Hill Cemetery, Niagara Falls, Ontario.

Maria Spelterini:
Crossing Niagara Wearing Peach Baskets

37

The year 1876 was a special one for the United States. The country was celebrating its centennial and all across the land, in communities large and small, special commemorative events were scheduled.

However, the main focus was on Philadelphia where the Declaration of Independence had been drafted and signed. That city hosted a huge international Centennial Exhibition which attracted some 10 million visitors during its six-month run.

In Niagara Falls, New York, excitement was running high during the first part of July 1876, since, as part of that community's centennial celebrations, a talented tightrope walker was giving a series of thrilling performances high over the Niagara River Gorge.

Maria Spelterini was the only woman tightrope walker to perform at Niagara Falls. Here, wearing peach baskets on her feet, she makes her way across the rope during one of her July 1876 performances. The Railway Suspension Bridge, crowded with spectators, is in the background.

Sherman Zavitz Collection.

Although this type of show had been seen at Niagara before (the first such performer here was the great Blondin in 1859 and 1860), now, for the first time, the artist was a woman.

Her name was Maria Spelterini. Not only did she prove herself equal to her male predecessors on the rope, but she undoubtedly also struck a blow for the equality of women.

According to a background report published by the *New York Herald*, Maria hailed from Livorno, Italy, and made her first public appearance with her father's circus troupe when she was three years old. Later establishing a solo career, she achieved great renown as a tightrope artist in a number of European cities. The paper noted, "She is gifted with wonderful nerve combined with cool daring."

These traits were certainly evident during her shows at Niagara Falls, the first of which took place on July 8, 1876. Her rope was stretched across the gorge at a point just below the Railway Suspension Bridge, which was situated where the Whirlpool Rapids Bridge is now.

The Niagara Falls, New York, *Gazette* provided a brief but interesting account of Maria's July 8 performance, although the paper was obviously more taken with her appearance than with what she actually did on the rope. It reported:

"The Signorina made the across and return trips attired in flesh coloured tights, a tunic of scarlet, a sea-green bodice and neat green buskins (boots). The lady is twenty-three years of age, with dark Italian features, superbly built and weighing in the neighbourhood of a hundred and fifty pounds. She made no attempt to walk against time, merely traveling the gossamer web with a graceful, confident step, which soon allayed all apprehension of impending disaster."

Tremendous crowds (many people stood on the Suspension Bridge) were on hand to watch each of her shows and Maria thrilled them with exciting stunts on the rope. For example, she crossed with her arms and legs shackled in chains and then with a paper bag over her head. On one occasion she walked forward from the American to the Canadian side and returned walking backwards without once turning around. Another time she skipped across the 300-metre (1000-foot)-long rope.

In what became one of her more famous routines, Maria crossed with peach baskets on her feet. Always attired in a colorful, showy costume, she frequently wore a flat hat set at a jaunty angle.

From Niagara Falls, Maria went on to perform at the Centennial Exhibition in Philadelphia. After that, she dropped out of sight. Despite research efforts by a number of people, not even the year or place of her death has so far been discovered – adding a note of mystery to Niagara's only female tightrope walker.

Reginald Fessenden: A Father of AM Radio's Niagara Connection

38

One of the most significant events in the history of communication took place on Christmas Eve, 1906. It was the world's first radio broadcast. The genius behind this landmark scientific achievement was a man who had spent a good portion of his youth in what is now Niagara Falls. His name was Reginald Aubrey Fessenden.

Born in 1866 at East Bolton, Quebec, Reginald moved to Niagara Falls (then known as Clifton) at the age of 10 when his father, Elisha, became rector at Christ Church on River Road.

After arriving here, Reginald was able to obtain, through a scholarship, admittance as a day student to the DeVeaux Military School in Niagara Falls, New York. Early each day, except

Reginald Fessenden, one of the fathers of AM radio, spent a good portion of his youth in Niagara Falls, Ontario.

From *Fessenden: Builder of Tomorrows* (1940).

Sunday, he would leave the church rectory, at that time located on Cataract Avenue, and trudge across the Suspension Bridge (now the site of the Whirlpool Rapids Bridge), returning in the late afternoon.

After a year at DeVeaux, Reginald was sent to Trinity College School, a private school for boys at Port Hope, Ontario. A very precocious student, he thoroughly enjoyed his years at Trinity.

Holidays were spent in Niagara Falls and certainly few youngsters loved exploring the Niagara Rivet as much as Reginald and his friends. He came to know it, understand it and respect it. Recalling his youth years later, he wrote: "We scrambled about the cliffs of the gorge between the Falls and the Whirlpool or at the Whirlpool. There was an old millrace, abandoned, just above the Whirlpool Rapids where we went in swimming; perfectly safe, but a very swift current so we were all strong swimmers. Closer to the Falls we could fish for eels and explore a cave where real smugglers and criminals hid when trying to get across the border."

He also enjoyed spending time at Dufferin Islands, as they are now called, where he could "lie along the grass next to the edge of the running water with a couple of good books to read."

In 1879, the Fessenden family moved upriver a bit to Chippawa where Elisha became the rector of Holy Trinity Church, a position he occupied for the next 14 years. Reginald later wrote warmly of this spot, especially the "delightful old rectory," which stood immediately south of the church.

Following eye surgery during 1881, Reginald was sent, for a year, to what is now known as Stamford Collegiate in Niagara Falls. He then returned to Trinity College.

Following his graduation, he both lectured and took classes at Bishop's University in Lennoxville, Quebec. However, he left Bishop's before obtaining a degree to take a teaching position in Bermuda. On his first day there, he met the daughter of a prominent planter. Her name was Helen May Trott and she would later become his wife.

Fessenden was by now a bearded, broad-shouldered giant of a man with an incredible mental output matched only by his great physical energy. Although he enjoyed Bermuda, he soon grew restless and after two years left for New York City. Determined to pursue a career in science, he wanted to see if he could get a job with the renowned Thomas Edison.

He was hired by Edison in 1886 and rose to the position of chief chemist before bankruptcy closed the inventor's laboratory four years later. During those years, Fessenden learned a great deal about electricity, something he felt was essential in order to achieve what had become his main goal – the transmission of the human voice without wires.

In September 1890, he and Helen were married in New York City and then, like many honeymooners before and since, came to Niagara Falls, staying with his parents at the Chippawa rectory. The parishioners quickly fell in love with "Mrs. Reggie," as some of them called Helen.

Fessenden then returned to teaching, first at Purdue University and later as a professor of electrical engineering at the University of Pittsburgh.

At the same time, the experiments with wireless continued. Then came a momentous day. On December 23, 1900, while working at his experimental wireless telegraphy station near Washington, Reginald sent his assistant, Alfred Thiessen, to the top of a 15-metre (49-foot)-high tower while he went to the transmitting shack of another tower 1.5 kilometres (nearly a mile) away. After starting his steam engine generator, Reginald spoke "Is it snowing where you are Mr. Thiessen? If it is, telegraph back and let me know."

Thiessen did hear and Reginald was soon grabbing his pen to write, "This afternoon...intelligible speech by electromagnetic waves has, for the first time in the world's history, been transmitted."

By 1906, Fessenden, with the backing of several millionaires, had built two transmission/receiving towers, one near Boston and the other on the west coast of Scotland. In January of that year, he made the first two-way Morse code transmission across the Atlantic. A few months later he accidentally achieved the first trans-Atlantic voice transmission.

On Christmas Eve 1906, Fessenden, with the help of Helen and his assistants, produced the world's first radio broadcast. It featured the playing of Handel's *Largo* on an Edison phonograph, several readings and Fessenden performing *O Holy Night* on his violin. Ships that had been equipped with radio receivers picked up the program as far away as the Caribbean Sea.

In the succeeding years, Fessenden turned his brilliant mind to a host of inventions. Some of these, such as the sonic depth finder and radio sonar, were designed to increase the safety of ships at sea. In 1919, he developed an early television apparatus. In all, he was responsible for some 500 inventions.

Reginald Fessenden died July 22, 1932, at his estate in Bermuda, far away from the Niagara River he had known and loved as a young man. He well deserves to be called one of the Fathers of AM Radio.

Lorne and Louise: The Governor-General and Victoria's Daughter

39

On March 21, 1871, a wedding of particular interest to Great Britain took place at St. George's Chapel in Windsor Castle.

The beautiful Princess Louise, daughter of Queen Victoria and the late Prince Albert, married the Marquis of Lorne, son of the Duke and Duchess of Argyll. It was a glittering affair. The scene, as one observer wrote, was "superb, full of pomp, music, pageantry and sunshine."

The newlyweds immediately became the darlings of the British public. Seven years later, this continuing popularity was one factor that prompted British Prime Minister Disraeli to invite Lorne to become the next Governor-General of Canada. He also felt that having Louise in Canada would improve the prestige of the Queen's representative there. Eagerly accepting, Lorne and his wife set sail for the young Dominion in mid-November 1878.

The popular Marquis of Lorne, Canada's Governor-General, and his wife, Princess Louise (the couple in the foreground), enjoying the view of Niagara Falls from Prospect Point on the American side, January 1879.

From *Illustrated London News*, February 1879. Sherman Zavitz Collection.

The appointment created a great deal of excitement in Canada. Not only was the Marquis of Lorne to be the new Governor-General, but the idea of having a member of the royal family also living in Ottawa's Rideau Hall, the official residence of the Governor-General, was, for most, a thrilling bonus.

Lorne and Louise had been settled in Ottawa for only a little over six weeks when they took their first out-of-town trip, a visit to Niagara Falls.

They arrived by train at 3:30 p.m. on January 21, 1879. As it was an unofficial visit, there was no formal welcome or any other ceremony during their four days at Niagara. Lorne, Louise and their entourage stayed at the Prospect House Hotel, which was owned by David Isaacs. It was located near Table Rock in what is now Queen Victoria Park, named for Louise's mother.

The area press eagerly reported on the activities as well as the appearance of the popular couple. Louise seemed to receive greater attention. A Buffalo paper, after noting how "very attractive" the princess was, then gave a complete description of her clothes, including her shoes: "Her size is number three and her foot is very pretty."

Niagara impressed the new Governor-General. In a letter written a week later back in Ottawa, he recalled, "There was so much ice about the falls that the sound of the water was a little hushed by the curtains of icicles and the mountains of ice piled on the rocks below the falls. But the effect of the whole in winter is marvelously grand."

Lorne and Louise returned to Niagara for a few days in early September 1882. They were met at the Grand Trunk (now VIA Rail) Station on Bridge Street by David Isaacs, who again hosted them at his Prospect House. This visit was to provide it brief rest for the Vice-Regal couple before they began a journey to the Pacific coast. A Niagara Falls, New York, *Gazette* reporter at the Prospect House, noted that "the Governor-General was walking along the bank, while the Princess was seated in the balcony of Table Rock House sketching a portion of the Horseshoe Fall."

Lorne's term of office was up in the fall of 1883 and he and Louise returned to England. He had developed a great affection for Canada and its people and, therefore, was particularly saddened to leave because, according to an unwritten rule, former Governors-General could never return.

Louise, on the other hand, was anxious to go. While she had made a number of friends and admirers in Canada, she had not been able to fully adapt to either Ottawa's society or its cold winters. Consequently, she had taken several prolonged visits back to England and Europe during her husband's term as Governor-General. This always gave rise to rumours that their marriage was in trouble.

Lorne had reached his career zenith in Canada. He lived the rest of his life in England and Scotland, dying May 2, 1914, at the age of 68.

Louise passed away December 3, 1939, in London at the advanced age of 91.

They left their mark on Canada in a variety of ways. For example, the Princess gave her name to one of the most beautiful lakes in the Canadian Rockies, Lake Louise. As for Lorne, his name seemed to have great appeal, and for several generations following his departure, many baby boys in Canada were christened after the former Governor-General. In fact, no other country in the world once had so many men with Lorne as their given name.

"Endless Water Falling the Wrong Way": Oscar Wilde Does Niagara

40

Niagara Falls is "endless water falling the wrong way." This was one of a number of observations about the famous Falls made by the nineteenth-century author and wit, Oscar Wilde.

Born in Ireland in 1854, he studied classics at Oxford before settling in London and launching a writing career.

Throughout his adult years he continued the bohemian life style he had developed as a youth and preached a philosophy based on pleasure and beauty. Something of a dandy, he became famous for wearing long hair, a velvet jacket, knee breeches and black stockings, while often carrying a sunflower or lily. People found him outrageous, but at the same time vastly entertaining. He became a great favourite of many in British society for his sharp wit, flair and brilliant conversation.

A portrait of Oscar Wilde, around the time of his visit to Niagara in 1882.

From Lloyd Lewis and Henry Justin Smith, *Oscar Wilde Discovers America* (1936).

By the early 1880s, Wilde had become such a popular figure that a North American lecture tour was arranged. He arrived in New York on January 2, 1882. On hand to greet him was a horde of reporters anxious to interview a man who could come up with clever, quotable comments on just about anyone and anything. For example, on being asked by a customs official if he had anything to declare, Wilde replied, "Nothing but my genius."

Over the next ten months, he lectured in 140 cities across the United States and eastern Canada. It turned out to be a highly successful tour.

On the afternoon of Wednesday, February 8, 1882, Wilde appeared at the Academy of Music in Buffalo. Following his lecture, he took a train to Niagara Falls, New York, where he spent the night at the Prospect House Hotel. The following day, wearing a long fur coat and derby hat, he set out to explore Niagara. The press followed along, hanging onto his every word.

The Niagara Falls, New York *Gazette* described him as "fully six feet tall and well proportioned. The features of his smoothly shaved face are strongly drawn... while his whole appearance presents that of a robust, hearty and well fed young Englishman." His only "peculiarity," the reporter felt, was his long, heavy hair, which was the colour of "old gold."

Wilde first expressed disappointment with Niagara Falls, commenting that the outline was "wanting in grandeur and variety of line." He was more charitable when he stood at the foot of the Falls under Table Rock. It was there he "realized the majestic splendour and strength of the physical force of nature. The sight was far beyond what I had ever seen in Europe." Wilde then quoted Leonardo da Vinci: "'The two most wonderful things in the world are a woman's smile and the motion of mighty waters.'"

Probably his most memorable comment about Niagara concerned honeymooners. He noted: "Every American bride is taken there, and the sight of the stupendous waterfall must be one of the earliest if not the keenest disappointments in American married life." A popular paraphrase of this comment is: "Niagara Falls must be a bride's second greatest disappointment."

Returning to England, Wilde continued his writing, lecturing and socializing. In 1884 he married Constance Lloyd. The couple had two sons.

His literary career reached its zenith in the early 1890s with the writing and production of a number of very successful stage plays.

Then in 1895, only a few weeks after the opening of his immensely popular *The Importance of Being Earnest,* he found himself the central figure in a scandal.

Wilde was publicly accused of having performed homosexual acts. He countered by launching a libel action. The case, and subsequent trial, created a sensation in Victorian Britain. Wilde was eventually convicted of gross indecency and sentenced to two years of hard labour.

He emerged from prison with his marriage and career in ruins. Three years of self-imposed exile in Europe followed. He died on November 30, 1900, in an obscure Paris hotel.

Oscar Wilde's brilliance, flamboyant life-style, great popularity and shattering fall were the ingredients of a life that will long be remembered. The Wilde legend lives on.

During his visit to Niagara Falls, Oscar Wilde wrote this inscription in the autograph album of David Isaacs, who was the proprietor of the Prospect House in Niagara Falls, New York.

It reads: "The roar of these waters is like the roar when 'The mighty wave democracy breaks on the shores where kings lie couched at ease.'"

Local History Department, Niagara Falls, New York, Public Library.

Captain Matthew Webb's Last Swim

Captain Matthew Webb lost his life while attempting to swim the Whirlpool Rapids in July 1883.
From *Tugby's Illustrated Guide to Niagara Falls* (1885). Sherman Zavitz Collection.

On any list of great 19th-century long-distance swimmers, the name of Captain Matthew Webb would have to be placed at or near the top. He also played a significant role in the Niagara story.

Born in Shropshire (now Salop), England, in 1848, Webb ran away to sea as a boy, eventually becoming the captain of a trading ship.

He first attracted public attention in 1873 by jumping from the Cunard steamer *Russia* during a wild storm to rescue a sailor who had been washed overboard. For this act of bravery he was awarded the Royal Humane Society's first gold medal.

On August 24-25, 1875, Captain Webb became the first person to swim across the English Channel, covering the 40 kilometres (25 miles) between Dover and Calais in 21 hours and 45 minutes. This accomplishment earned him $25,000 in prize money.

In 1882, Webb and his family moved to Boston so he could take part in various long-distance swimming events in the eastern United States. Feeling very confident of his ability, as well as looking for a new and novel challenge, Webb announced in the early summer of 1883 that he planned to swim through the Whirlpool Rapids of the Niagara River. The date eventually fixed for the attempt was July 24.

This was something that had never been done. Webb was well aware of the immense danger involved, but as he admitted to it *Toronto Globe* (now *Globe and Mail*) reporter just before the swim, "I am doing it because no other man has ever made the attempt. I am determined that my reputation shall not suffer." When asked about the greatest point of danger, Webb replied that he felt it was at the entrance to the Whirlpool. He also realized that he would often be forced under the water and frankly conceded, "The question is can I keep conscious till I get back on the surface?"

Summing up the interview, the reporter felt that the captain, whom he describes as nearly six feet (1.8 metres) tall and weighing 86 kilograms (190 pounds), spoke with "all the confidence bred of success."

The Whirlpool Rapids is one of the most ferocious stretches of white water in the world. In Webb's time there was twice as much water flowing through this section of the river since there were no diversions being made above the Falls for hydro-electric generation. The depth of the water in the rapids is presently estimated to be 12 metres (40 feet), while the current travels at about 48 kilometres (30 miles) an hour. This speed is partly due to the narrowness of the gorge, but mostly because the river drops 16 metres (52 feet) through this short section. The rapids themselves are caused by many large blocks of dolomite limestone that have tumbled into the gorge over thousands of years. As Webb noted just before his swim, "There is no place in the world like it and I am trusting to fortune."

At 3:30 p.m. on July 24, 1883, the captain left the Clifton House Hotel (now the site of Oakes Garden Theatre), walked down to the river's edge and got into a waiting boat. He was rowed out into the river by John McCloy, a well-known ferryman here at the time, who had been hired to take the swimmer downriver to the starting point. McCloy asked Webb how much prize money he still had from his English Channel swim. When the captain replied that $15,000 was left, McCloy reportedly said, "Let me pull you ashore and go and spend the remainder before you try this."

Captain Webb was not to be dissuaded, however, and when the boat reached a point about 400 metres (a quarter of a mile) above the Suspension Bridge (now the site of the Whirlpool Rapids Bridge), he dove into the water. McCloy gazed after him for a moment and then turned his boat around and headed back to the dock. It was 4:25.

There was not a huge crowd on hand to watch the attempt, partly because many people were convinced it wouldn't take place. Around 500 persons were on the bridge and a scattering of others were on the upper banks. When they saw Webb start the swim, there was intense excitement.

Webb's journey through the rapids was an extraordinary sight. At times he was seen above the water, at other times he was buried by it. Occasionally swimming with strong strokes, but often helpless in the raging torrent, Webb was swept into the Whirlpool, still alive, only about five minutes after he had passed under the Suspension Bridge. Here, as he had predicted, came the most critical moment of

Dr. Hodge:
A Nightmare on the Bridge

For over 150 years an important part of the Niagara story has centred around the bridges across the Niagara Gorge. The first of these was the Niagara Suspension Bridge, which opened in 1848. It was located where the Whirlpool Rapids Bridge now stands.

The first Upper Suspension Bridge, near the site of the present Rainbow Bridge, was built in 1869. Eighteen years later, work was begun to strengthen and widen this span.

The long and expensive project had been completed for only two months when there

The ruins of the Upper Suspension Bridge. In service only two months, it was destroyed during a vicious windstorm on January 9-10, 1889.

Local History Department, Niagara Falls, New York, Public Library.

came a fateful day, Wednesday January 9, 1889. On that evening a vicious windstorm roared into the Niagara area. By midnight it had increased in fury and became so violent that it snapped a fastening connected to one of the bridge's principal storm stays. This sealed its doom and over the next few hours the structure gradually came apart as the suspenders (the wires that connected the platform with the cables) began to detach.

At about ten o'clock that night, Dr. J.W. Hodge, of Niagara Falls, New York, had walked across the bridge to visit a patient on the Canadian side. Around 11:30 he began the return trip. By this time the wind was roaring down the gorge at almost hurricane speed, carrying both spray and sheeted water from the Falls.

Part way across, the doctor noticed, to his horror, that the bridge had broken away from some of its stays. It began surging up and down a good 6 metres (20 feet) and tipping sideways to an angle of 45 degrees. With freezing fingers he clung to the railing and picked his way across, fearing for his life every second.

The icy, sheeting water slammed into his face, almost blinding him, while the wind got under his overcoat and nearly tore the buttons off. He thought of ridding himself of the coat, but abandoned the idea when he realized that to take either hand off the railing would mean the wind could carry him away.

The intense cold, clashing wires, icy water and the upheaving and swinging back and forth of the bridge combined to create a nightmare almost beyond imagination for the doctor.

He continued to hold on and grope his way across. Eventually, exhausted, soaked and covered with ice, he reached the other side. At around 3:30 that morning the bridge gave one final mighty heave and crashed into the gorge below.

Dr. Hodge had been the last person to cross the bridge. Considering the ordeal he had been through, however, he no doubt considered that it was a distinction he could have just as well done without.

John Birchall:
Swindler and Murderer

44

Mrs. Baldwin's boarding house, where John Birchall was apprehended, was located on St. Clair Avenue next to St. Andrew's Church in downtown Niagara Falls.

John Burtniak Collection.

Niagara Falls played a prominent part in one of the most notorious and publicized crimes in nineteenth-century Ontario.

The story begins in London, England, with the elopement of John Reginald Birchall and Florence Stevenson during the early fall of 1888. Shortly after, the couple set sail for North America. Following a stay in New York City, they visited Niagara Falls and by the end of the year were boarding in Woodstock, Ontario, about 137 kilometres (85 miles) to the west of Niagara.

By this time their finances were almost depleted. In order to improve their credit status, they passed themselves off as members of the British upper class, calling themselves Lord and Lady Somerset.

Pretending that they wished to purchase land, the Birchalls made many trips through the countryside, becoming familiar figures in the region. On one of these excursions, the couple came across an almost impenetrable area known as the Blenheim Swamp. They made a number of visits to this spot, which was to play an important role in future events.

In the spring of 1889, the Birchalls suddenly vanished from Woodstock, leaving many unpaid bills behind.

Back in England, John Birchall began developing an elaborate swindle. He placed an advertisement in several London newspapers. It stated that he owned a farm near Niagara Falls, Ontario, and wished to meet a "gentleman's son" to go and live with him on the farm and learn the business. If everything worked out, a partnership would be offered. Before being accepted, an initial fee of 500 pounds had to be paid to cover lodging and the purchase of more stock. Future investments would also be required.

Two men, Douglas Pelly and Frederick Benwell, responded to the ad. Birchall interviewed each separately and painted a glowing picture of his Niagara farm which, of course, was completely non-existent.

Both young men paid their first installment money, but it was only when they and the Birchalls were ready to set sail for New York that Pelly and Benwell met each other and found out that both were going to Niagara for the same reason. Since there was to be only one investor, Pelly was furious and went to Birchall threatening to withdraw from the arrangement. Birchall pacified him, saying that at some point he would find a way to get rid of Benwell.

The foursome crossed the Atlantic and reached Buffalo on February 16, 1890. It was decided that Mrs. Birchall would wait there until she knew everything was ready for her at the farm. Pelly was asked to stay with her while Birchall and Benwell took a train for Niagara early the next morning.

Late that night, Birchall returned to Buffalo alone. He stated that Benwell had not liked the farm, had been given the addresses of some neighbours to visit, and then gone on his way.

In fact, Birchall had taken the unsuspecting Benwell beyond Niagara Falls. They got off the train at Eastwood, which was near Woodstock and the desolate Blenheim Swamp, an area Birchall knew well. Benwell was escorted into the marsh, while being told that just beyond it he would see the magnificent farm to which he had tied his future. Instead, he met a sudden, violent death as Birchall whipped out a revolver and pumped two bullets into the back of the young man's head. He then emptied Bendwell's pockets and cut out all clothing labels. The plan was to dump the body into a supposedly bottomless part of the bog called Pine Pond. Since Birchall's last visit to the area, however, storm damage had cut off access to this spot, so he simply hid the body under some brush. Returning to the station, he then took a train back to Buffalo.

The next day, the Birchalls and Pelly came to Niagara Falls, Ontario, and took rooms at Baldwin's boarding house on St. Clair Avenue, on the present-day site of the office building behind the post office.

Birchall now plotted to get rid of Pelly. On one occasion, as they were walking across the Railway Suspension Bridge, he encouraged Pelly to lean far over the railing to view the rapids. But just as he was beginning to make a move to push him over into the river, a pedestrian approached, spoiling his attempt.

Pelly's suspicions were aroused, however, and from that point on he carried a gun with him and was constantly looking over his shoulder.

John Birchall – scan artist and murderer.
Sherman Zavitz Collection.

Frederick Benwell – victim.
Sherman Zavitz Collection.

On February 21, two brothers, who were chopping wood in the Blenheim Swamp, stumbled across Benwell's body. The find was reported to authorities, who in turn called in John Wilson Murray, the Ontario Department of Justice's chief detective. Murray was the most famous policeman in Canada and was noted for being far ahead of his time in scientific criminal detection.

Finding no clue to identify the victim, Murray had Benwell's picture taken and published in various newspapers, asking anyone who recognized him to report it to the police. Pelly saw the picture and urged the Birchalls to go to Woodstock and make the identification. Feeling cornered, they did so, and while there Murray questioned them carefully. As Florence paced the floor, Birchall claimed they had met Benwell on board the ship and then, after travelling to Niagara together, the victim had gone on to London, Ontario, to buy land. Murray was suspicious of the Birchalls and as they returned to Niagara Falls, telegraphed local authorities there to put a surveillance on them.

The great detective continued his investigation, which included interviews with Pelly and the train crews for February 17, the day Benwell disappeared. He soon had enough evidence to have Birchall charged with murder. The arrest took place in Niagara Falls on March 2, 1890. His wife was arrested two days later, but was subsequently released due to lack of evidence.

Birchall's preliminary hearing was held in the Niagara Falls Town Hall, which was located in front of the present City Hall. There was great excitement in the streets and crowds gathered around the building to await the outcome. He was committed for trial and sent to Woodstock.

The trial began on September 22, 1890, and was covered by reporters from newspapers all over Canada, the United States, England and a number of European countries.

John Birchall was found guilty. He was hanged in the Woodstock jail yard on the cold, grey morning of November 14, 1890. His days as a swindler and murderer had come to a dramatic end.

Arthur Hoyt Day: Murder at Niagara

45

For the vast majority of the countless millions of visitors who have come to Niagara over the years, the trip has been made in order to enjoy the great beauty, majesty and history of the area. Arthur Hoyt Day, however, had no such reason for his visit. He came here with murder on his mind.

On Sunday, July 27, 1890, the 26-year-old Day, along with his wife, Desire, and his sister, Mary Quigley, travelled by train from their Rochester, New York, home to Niagara for, as the two ladies were told, a day of sightseeing.

The Welland County Court House and Jail in Welland at the turn of the 20th century. It was here that Arthur Hoyt Day's trial was held.

John Burtniak Collection.

After arriving in Niagara Falls, New York, the trio crossed the Railway Suspension Bridge and began walking along the Canadian side of the river towards the Whirlpool.

According to Mary Quigley's later testimony, she eventually became tired and sat down on a rock to rest while her brother and Desire walked on a bit further. She could see Day with his wife immediately in front of him, standing a short distance away at the very edge of the gorge. Her attention was then drawn to something else for a moment, and when she next looked for her brother and sister-in-law, she saw only Arthur. He was waving a black handkerchief and motioning for her to come over to him. Desire was nowhere in sight.

When she reached him, Day quickly and calmly admitted he had pushed his wife over the bank because "he wanted to get rid of her." Telling his sister not to go to the police, he handed her a train ticket to get home and then disappeared. When she next saw him three days later back in Rochester, he told her he was feeling only some regret for what he had done.

What Mary Quigley did not know, however, was that 15 days before the Niagara trip, Arthur had married a Lizzie Breen when, as he later admitted, they were both drunk. Since then he had been maintaining two households. Realizing this arrangement could not last long, Day apparently decided that Desire, his wife of eight years, had to go. He then organized the fateful excursion to Niagara Falls.

After his return, however, Lizzie began having some concerns about her new husband. For one thing, he kept talking in his sleep, saying such things as, "There she goes over." She also began hearing rumours that he was already married.

Lizzie finally went to the police, who soon after arrested Day for bigamy. Now a large problem arose since Desire could not be found. When the police questioned Mary Quigley, however, she broke her silence and told the story of the July 27 trip.

She was then brought back to Niagara Falls. On August 10 Mary took American and local authorities to the spot along the gorge where Desire had been pushed over the edge. After a difficult search, the victim's body, badly decomposed, was found on the rocks below. Arthur Hoyt Day was then extradited and charged with murder. He was taken to Welland, about 32 kilometres (20 miles) west of Niagara Falls, and lodged in the county jail there.

Arthur Hoyt Day, who had an appointment with the hangman on December 18, 1890.

From Welland *Tribune*, December 19, 1890.

The trial was held on October 8, 1890, in Welland. The case had created such a sensation that the courtroom was jammed with spectators, and hundreds of others who had hoped to watch the proceedings had to be turned away.

Day appeared impeccably dressed, including a red flower in his coat lapel. He pleaded not guilty.

The Crown's case rested largely on the testimony of Mary Quigley, while the defence tried its best to discredit her testimony because of her past. Mary, who was described by the press as "hard-looking," had been married four times, arrested on numerous occasions, and had at one time been the madam in a Lockport, New York brothel.

For his part, Day said that he and Desire had quarrelled after reaching the Canadian side of the river, had parted company, and he hadn't seen her since. Later, his story changed and he testified that she had slipped while trying to pick some berries. He never could explain, however, why he had not reported her lengthy disappearance or accident.

The 12-man jury brought in a guilty verdict. The judge pronounced the death sentence and directed that Day "be taken from the prison where you are now confined on December 18, and hanged by the neck until you are dead, and may the Lord have mercy on your soul."

The hanging took place on gallows set up outside the courthouse on East Main Street in Welland. As the *Welland Tribune* reported: "About seventy persons witnessed the execution, Niagara Falls town being especially well represented. The wind was raw and whilst waiting for the grievesome event many kept warm by vigorous marching and counter marching."

Day, smartly dressed as always with the usual flower in his lapel, was led to the gallows at 7:55 a.m. He maintained his innocence to the end, accusing his sister of having lied at the trial and being the one really responsible for Desire's death. His arms had already been pinioned and now his legs were bound and the black cape pulled over his head. At exactly 7:57, as the Lord's Prayer was being recited by the officiating minister, the drop was released.

As the *Tribune* later noted, "Arthur Hoyt Day had paid a fearful penalty for a fearful crime."

122

Mrs. Grimason: An "Escape from a Terrible Death"

46

The Upper Suspension Bridge, pictured here in 1892, was the scene of a dramatic rescue on September 24th of that year. The view is looking toward the Canadian side of the Niagara River, with the Clifton House Hotel visible at the extreme left.

Sherman Zavitz Collection.

It was Saturday, September 24, 1892. Among the many visitors in Niagara Falls that day were several hundred delegates attending the Pan-Presbyterian convention in Toronto. A day's outing to Niagara had been arranged for them and the large group had arrived by special train that morning.

One of the delegates was Rev. Ramsey from Ireland who was accompanied on the Niagara excursion by a Mrs. Grimason who was a family friend and her two daughters, all of Toronto.

After strolling through Queen Victoria Park, the foursome crossed the Upper Suspension Bridge to have a closer look at the American Falls and to visit Goat Island. This bridge, which was just upstream from the current Rainbow Bridge, had been constructed in 1889.

Around 3 p.m., Rev. Ramsey, Mrs. Grimason and her daughters began to walk back across the bridge to Canada, with the minister and the young ladies in the lead. Suddenly, Rev. Ramsey heard a strange noise behind him. Looking back, he was shocked to see that Mrs. Grimason had disappeared, with just her parasol lying on the bridge to show where she had been only a moment before.

Peering over the railing. Ramsey saw the unfortunate lady wedged between one of the deck supports and a gas pipe just under the bridge.

Without hesitation, Ramsey climbed over the railing and, using one of the bridge cables, slid down to Mrs. Grimason. He then tried his best to comfort the frantic woman as she hung precariously some 60 metres (200 feet) above the rocks at the river's edge.

Several people in the large crowd that had gathered ran to get help. Harry Williams from the nearby Clifton House Hotel (now the site of Oakes Garden Theatre) and Harry Huntly, a foreman with the Niagara Falls, New York, Electric Light Company, quickly arrived on the scene.

After a rope was lowered over the railing, they went down to join Rev. Ramsey. While the three men were carefully getting a rope around the lady, her gold watch fell to the rocks below where it was smashed to bits – a chilling reminder of what one false move could mean to any of the four individuals involved in this life-and-death drama. After what seemed like hours, the rope was finally in place and, amid the cheers of the crowd, Mrs. Grimason was pulled to safety and the embraces of her daughters.

She was immediately taken to the Clifton House to be examined. While badly shaken from the ordeal, it was found that she had not suffered any serious physical injury. Harry Williams, who had played the leading role in the daring rescue, was hailed as a hero and was later awarded a medal for bravery.

In recounting what had happened, Mrs. Grimason stated that she had tripped while walking on the bridge's narrow sidewalk and had fallen through an opening in the railing. Striking one of the bridge cables or suspenders, she was thrown inward, causing her to become trapped between the deck support and the gas pipe. Those in the crowd who were familiar with the bridge realized that if the accident had happened a bit closer to the Canadian side, it would have meant certain death since the gas pipe gradually sloped away from the bridge.

The iron railing on the south side of the bridge, the only side that had a walkway, was close to 1.5 metres (5 feet) high but just had a single rail between the top and the bottom. This meant there were openings big enough even for a person like Mrs. Grimason, who was described as "tall and inclined to stoutness," to fall through.

The lucky lady had recovered sufficiently to return to Toronto on the 5 o'clock train that afternoon.

Her experience added another chapter of high drama and courage to the Niagara story. As the local press wrote: "There have been many strange scenes witnessed at Niagara Falls, but this was the strangest and most affecting ever witnessed by old residents. The escape from a terrible death was miraculous, and Mrs. Grimason will never remember without a thrill of horror when she hung between life and death over the terrible chasm of the Niagara River, with its cruel rocks and restless waters."

Helen Keller:
An Extraordinary Woman Visits Niagara

47

Helen Keller, a remarkable
woman who was able to
experience the mighty Niagara,
despite her overwhelming disabilities.

From Helen Keller, *The Story of My Life*
(1903).

The name Helen Keller will always be associated with a remarkable woman's inspiring battle and ultimate victory against overwhelming disabilities.

Born on June 27, 1880, in Tuscumbia, Alabama, a prolonged high fever left Helen both blind and deaf when she was only 19 months old.

In 1887, the Keller family hired 21-year-old Anne Sullivan as a live-in teacher for Helen. Anne was able to reach the little girl as no one else had and taught her how to cope with life in a dark and soundless world. Helen was eventually able to make a brilliant success of her life, to the point where it seemed she had been virtually freed from her limitations. This was due to her own determination and intelligence, as well as Anne's excellent teaching and lengthy compassionate friendship.

Helen learned to read using the Braille system and to write using a special typewriter. She also learned to speak.

In March 1893, Helen, along with Anne and Alexander Graham Bell, who had become a good friend of Helen's, made a trip to upstate New York. Bell, although famous as the inventor of the telephone, was primarily a teacher of the deaf, and wanted Helen to visit a school for the deaf in Rochester.

While there Helen and Dr. Bell made travel arrangements to visit Niagara Falls, partly as a surprise treat for Anne, or "Teacher," as Helen usually called her. Bell himself was unable to make the trip, so his friend, Edmund Lyon and Mrs. A.C. Pratt, an assistant of Dr. Bell's from Boston, accompanied the young ladies.

To most visitors it is a combination of the sight and sound of Niagara that is so awe-inspiring and leaves such a lasting impression. Therefore, it seems fair to wonder how Helen, both blind and deaf, could understand or appreciate a visit to Niagara Falls. Yet, the trip here was a great success.

Helen had learned the concepts of distance and space and, therefore, she did come to comprehend the size and even the appearance of the Falls after she had explored them in a variety of ways.

They stayed at a hotel in Niagara Falls, New York, that was located right beside the river so she could feel the rush of the water by simply putting her hand on the window. Dr. Bell had also given her a down pillow which she could hold against herself to increase the vibrations.

In a letter written to her mother several weeks later, Helen noted a problem many persons with all their senses intact have had when trying to describe Niagara Falls. She wrote: "I wish I could describe the cataract as it is, its beauty and awful grandeur, and the fearful and irresistible plunge of its waters over the brow of the precipice. One feels helpless and overwhelmed in the presence of such a vast force." Obviously, only someone who had been profoundly affected by Niagara's power and beauty could write those words.

She also mentions in the letter how they "went down a hundred and twenty feet in an elevator that we might see the violent eddies and whirlpools in the deep gorge below the Falls."

Finally, in order for Helen to experience something of the width of the gorge, they travelled to the Ontario side of the river. She wrote: "When we crossed over to the Canadian side, I cried, 'God save the Queen!' Teacher said I was a little traitor. But I do not think so. I was only doing as the Canadians do, while I was in their country and besides I honour England's good queen."

Helen Keller seemed to enjoy her stay here as much as any visitor ever has. In her mind there was no doubt she saw and heard Niagara Falls.

King Camp Gillette: Utopia at Niagara Falls

48

One early morning in Brookline, Massachusetts, back in 1895, a 40-year-old travelling salesman with a well-lathered face picked up his straight razor, looked into a mirror and began to shave.

He quickly stopped, however, when he realized the razor was too dull to do a proper job. It was even beyond stropping and would have to be taken to a barber for honing.

The frustrated shaver was King Camp Gillette, a man who had always dreamed of inventing something that would be needed by almost everyone and that would have to be purchased over and over.

As he stared at his straight razor that momentous morning, a picture of what we know today as the safety razor came into his mind. He later wrote, "I saw it all in a moment, and stood there in a trance of joy." This vision depicted a thin, uniform steel strip, with opposite edges sharpened and held in place with a clamp and handle.

A great deal of work and experimenting followed. It was 1903 before

King Camp Gillette, the inventor of the safety razor, was also a socialist who envisioned a Utopian city, "Metropolis", centered around Niagara Falls.

From King Camp Gillette, *The Human Drift* (1894).

he was able to market his new products, selling 51 razors and 168 blades that year. By 1917, he was selling a million razors and 120 million blades annually. Beards were rapidly disappearing.

King Camp Gillette was more than an inventor and salesman, however. He was also a Utopian socialist who believed that the competitive system brought about greed and waste. He concluded that society was ready for a great industrial change that would bring about economic order and efficiency. This would then create ideal social conditions and so a perfect world would be achieved. "Under a flawless economic system of production and distribution," Gillette wrote, "there can be only one city in North America and possibly in the world." Because of its unlimited natural source of power, he felt that the site of this city, which he named Metropolis, should be centred around Niagara Falls.

Metropolis would be a rectangular city, 72 kilometres (45 miles) by 217 kilometres (135 miles). It would stretch from just beyond Rochester, New York, in the east to Hamilton, Ontario, in the west and have an area of almost 15,540 square kilometres (6,000 square miles). The residential section of Metropolis would be in the western New York State area where he envisioned some 60 million people, virtually the entire population of the United States at that time, would live in thousands of 25-storey apartment buildings. All other cities would be abandoned.

The industrial district would be in Niagara Falls. He intended to use all the water for energy, actually destroying the Falls in the process. A logical and orderly system of production and distribution would be established. This would be achieved by each manufacturing industry having only one plant. Therefore there would be only one paper mill, one steel plant and so on for the whole continent. All the consumers and workers would be living nearby. With no competition and practically no transportation, distribution and marketing costs, Gillette reasoned that there would be a great deal of excess wealth. This money would be used to improve social conditions, creating equality in society. This achievement, in turn, would mean that problems like crime would be eliminated.

Gillette's Utopia was detailed in a book he wrote, titled *The Human Drift,* published in 1894, the year before his safety razor vision. None of his plans for Niagara ever materialized, of course. In fact, the very competitive system he criticized helped make it possible for him to earn a fortune with his safety razors and blades.

King Camp Gillette died in 1932, but thanks to the continuing success of the company he founded, his name is still a very well-known one in many parts of the world.

Gillette envisioned all of North America's population living in 25-storey apartment buildings in western New York State.
From King Camp Gillette, *The Human Drift* (1894).

128

Nikola Tesla:
Electrical History is Made at Niagara Falls 49

Standing in Queen Victoria Park close to Table Rock and the Horseshoe Falls, is a statue that honours a giant in the world of science. His name was Nikola Tesla and he also played an important role in the Niagara story.

Tesla was born in 1856 to Serbian parents in Croatia. His extraordinary mental ability was evident while still a boy. For example, he could solve difficult mathematical problems almost instantly

Statue of Nikola Tesla in Queen Victoria Park following a dusting of snow.

Photo by Andrew Porteus, Niagara Falls, Ontario, Public Library.

without using paper, while his photographic memory allowed him to master large volumes of information quickly and easily.

While still in primary school, an event occurred that foretold an important part of Tesla's destiny. As he was looking through an old book one day, he came across a steel engraving of Niagara Falls. It captured his imagination. As Tesla stared at the picture, he envisioned how a great wheel could be made to turn from the tremendous force of the water. Shortly after this, he reportedly told an uncle how one day he would go to America and harness the power of the Falls.

Although his parents assumed that their son would become a member of the clergy like his father, Nikola had other ideas and at the age of 19 entered the Technical University at Graz, Austria, to study electrical engineering.

While there, he began to think about the possibility of developing a substitute for direct current. This type of current had limited use since it only had a range of about 2.6 square kilometres (one square mile) from the point of generation. It wasn't long until Tesla became convinced that an alternating current motor was possible. However, nobody in the academic or scientific world believed him.

Several years later while walking through a Budapest park, he had a sudden flash of insight that revealed exactly how the motor should be constructed. The prototype he built a few months later worked perfectly. Tesla had not only devised the AC induction motor, as it came to be known, but had also discovered a new principle of electricity. Alternating current, based on a rotating magnetic field, would enable electricity to be transmitted efficiently over great distances.

Nevertheless, all this was radical thinking in Europe where the direct current system was considered the way to go. As a result, Tesla decided to try his luck in the United States. He arrived in New York City during the summer of 1884 with four cents in his pocket and a letter of introduction for Thomas Edison from one of the famous inventor's European associates who had met Tesla and recognized his genius.

Edison hired the young engineer to work in his laboratory but Tesla left less than a year later. Not only did Edison feel that alternating current was "nonsense," but a dispute arose between the two men over payment for some extra work Tesla had done.

Over the next few years, Tesla's fortunes hit rock bottom – for a while he had to take a job digging ditches just to survive. Then in early 1887 his luck changed. He found two wealthy backers to finance the formation of the Tesla Electric Company. Within months he had developed the machinery, dynamos, motors, transformers and distribution equipment necessary for alternating current. Patents were taken out on all aspects of the system.

Another stroke of luck developed when George Westinghouse, a prominent American inventor and businessman, became a supporter of alternating current. He bought Tesla's patents and hired him as a consultant at the phenomenal salary for the time of two thousand dollars a month.

In 1893, Westinghouse and Tesla demonstrated alternating current to the public for the first time at the World's Columbian Exposition in Chicago. That same year the Niagara Falls Power Company awarded the Westinghouse Corporation the contract to build the generators for a gigantic hydro-electric project already under way in Niagara Falls, New York. Tesla's childhood dream of harnessing Niagara's power was about to become a reality.

In the late evening of November 15, 1896, a remarkable event occurred. Buffalo began to receive electricity from the Niagara Falls Power Company's generating plant alongside the Niagara River in Niagara Falls, New York – 34 kilometres (21 miles) away. Never before had electricity on a large scale been transmitted such a distance. Tesla's alternating current system had made it possible. As well as a personal victory for the inventor, it was a great leap forward in the history of electrical generation since it was now clear that alternating current was a more practical means of providing power. As Tesla noted, the time had arrived when it was possible to "harness the energies of nature to the service of man."

Recognizing the significance of this discovery, the generating stations that were built on the Canadian side of the Niagara River in the early years of the 20th century also used alternating current.

During much of the 1890s, Nikola Tesla was the most celebrated scientist and inventor in the world. A brilliant and complex man with almost mystical abilities, he was also responsible for a host of other inventions including the Tesla coil, which is still used in radio and television sets. He died in 1943.

Along with the statue, there is, in another part of Queen Victoria Park, a plaque dedicated to Tesla. In addition, there is a large statue of the inventor on Goat Island. They all serve as a tribute to this remarkable man and remind us of his triumph at Niagara Falls.

Queen Victoria Park: A Picnic by the Falls

50

At one time, Queen Victoria Park had facilities for large picnics. During the 1890s, this elaborate, rather rustic-looking picnic pavillion was located in the park at the foot of Murray Hill.

Sherman Zavitz Collection.

"A better-looking and more orderly crowd never visited Niagara Falls."

This was the conclusion of the local press in describing the vast number of people that were picnicking in Queen Victoria Park on Wednesday, July 17, 1895.

The throng was made up primarily of various excursion groups, the biggest of which consisted of over 2,000 members of the Hamilton, Ontario, Retail Grocers' Association – it had taken 30 railway passenger cars to bring them here.

Also present, however, were the employees of a large Toronto company and a number of Sunday School classes from Fort Erie.

Park Superintendent James Wilson later estimated that between 8,000 and 10,000 people enjoyed a picnic by the Falls that day.

In its early years, Queen Victoria Park, which opened in 1888, was promoted as a place for picnics and every effort was made to provide the appropriate facilities for this kind of activity. For example, a special picnic area that included a large rustic-looking pavilion was established at the foot of Murray Hill, just north of Table Rock.

An account published in a London, Ontario, newspaper in 1895, provided some interesting details about how the park catered to picnics: "The picnic grounds furnish ample accommodations for several thousand people at the same time. Tables and seats are placed under the inviting shade of the spreading trees, while an abundance of cool spring water is at

The Hamilton Retail Grocers' Association held their annual picnic in Queen Victoria Park for many years. This is a scene from the 1906 version. A large crowd is watching some foot races. John Burtniak Collection.

hand in all directions. During the summer months, an officer is continuously engaged in preparing and supplying hot water for those who bring their own provisions and who desire to make their own tea and coffee.

"These and other privileges in the way of games – lacrosse, baseball, football, etc., are provided free of cost. Excursionists come and go and enjoy these advantages without the expenditure of a single cent, unless they find it desirable to patronize the restaurant which is conducted for the accommodation of those who bring no refreshments."

The restaurant referred to was the Dufferin Café. It was housed in the former Niagara Falls Museum building, which was located where Queen Victoria Place is now.

Of course, a bonus for all those having a picnic at the Falls was Queen Victoria Park's exceptionally beautiful appearance – a reputation it still enjoys today. The press, in reporting the picnic activities of July 17, 1895, called the park "a veritable tourists' paradise."

It went on to note: "The thousands who visited the park on Wednesday were loud in their praises of the flower beds that form such a beautiful foreground to the picnic grounds. Not a weed can be found to mar the beauty of the flowers and the lawns about them are shaven as clean and kept as green as the most aesthetic admirer could wish."

As an extra feature on that long-ago July day, there was a concert in the park presented at two o'clock by the XIII Battalion Band of Hamilton. Selections included the *William Tell Overature* and a minuet by Paderewski.

Queen Victoria Park no longer has picnic or recreational facilities. However, The Niagara Parks Commission provides a large number of picnic tables in many other areas as well as picnic pavilions at Queenston Heights Park, Old Fort Erie, McFarland Point Park, the Niagara Glen and King's Bridge Park.

A picnic along the Niagara River remains a popular summertime tradition for thousands of people.

A Stroll Across the Ice Bridge: "A Glorious Lark"

51

The ice bridge in the Niagara Gorge, immediately below the Falls, is a dramatic and popular winter wonder. This natural spectacle, which is much like a suspended glacier, forms almost every year and never fails to generate great interest from both visitors and residents.

At one time, it was a common practice to walk on the ice bridge. As a Niagara guidebook from 1896 commented: "As soon as considered safe,

In this circa 1905 photo, a stylishly dressed young woman poses on the ice bridge with a partially frozen American Falls in the background. Laura Bradshaw Durand had a "glorious lark" on the ice bridge in 1896.

Sherman Zavitz Collection.

paths are made from shore to shore and sometimes shanty restaurants and shelters are built in midstream." Wisely, a note of caution was included, with the author adding, "The river is carefully watched for signs of break-up, for once the ice goes, it goes with a rush. Woe be to any unhappy mortal carried down with it."

It was the desire to see Niagara Falls in its winter glory, and especially the ice bridge, that brought a Toronto *Globe* (now *Globe and Mail*) journalist here in mid-February 1896. Her name was Laura Bradshaw Durand, although she often wrote under the pseudonym "Pharos."

Born in Toronto and privately educated, she had joined the *Globe* in 1894 at the age of 29. Within a few years, Laura had earned considerable success as an editorial writer and a book reviewer. She also wrote features for young people.

Laura was invited to Niagara by the management of the Niagara Falls Park and River Railway, an electric line that had opened in 1893 between Chippawa and Queenston. She described her Niagara experience in a column entitled, "A Mid-Winter Lark" that was published in the *Globe* on February 22, 1896.

Accompanied by two friends she calls Miss Wiseacre and the Girl in the Red Dress, Laura travelled to Niagara Falls by train, arriving at the Grand Trunk (now VIA Rail) station on Bridge Street in the late morning.

Laura Bradshaw Durand (1865-1925) was a prominent Toronto journalist.

James A Gibson Library, Brock University, St. Catharines, Ontario.

The trio then walked across the street, which she describes as being ankle-deep in slush, and had a "well-served" lunch at the Rosli Hotel. This hotel, a well-known one for many years, was on Bridge Street near Cataract Avenue. It was at the Rosli that they also met the representative from the Niagara Falls Park and River Railway who was to act as their host and guide for the afternoon.

The "lieutenant," as she calls him, first escorted his guests to Table Rock. Stunned by the noise and fury, Laura wrote, "When we reached the brink of that surpassing water leap, the sleet was driving before the storm. We looked upon a chaotic world of monstrous form and sound, of terrifying force and chilling desolation." The "lieutenant" was delighted that she appreciated the scene since, as he told her, he had recently escorted several people to the same spot who, after gazing at the Falls, turned away quite unimpressed, asking, "'What else could the water do but go over?'"

Laura states the ice bridge was "stupendous" with an estimated depth of 12 metres (40 feet). She goes on to say, "Beneath this mass the raging river channels out a way and over it travellers walk merrily."

Laura and her friends became some of those "travellers." Standing below the Falls, they fell silent "before the expression of its majesty." In the middle of the ice bridge, as if mocking the elements, stood a rather frail, wooden booth with signs indicating that beef tea, cake and coffee were for sale there. Inside, next to a cozy stove, a man sat smoking. As Laura and her companions passed by "he grinned in salutation at his own novelty." At another shanty, an offer was made to take their tintype picture.

Throughout their ice bridge crossing, heavy volumes of spray from the Horseshoe Falls descended on them, so that by the time the threesome reached the American side they were almost drenched. Then came a grueling climb of 232 steps to reach the top of the gorge.

Still trying to dry out, Laura, Miss Wiseacre and the Girl in the Red Dress headed back to Toronto on the evening train. They were quite certain very few other visitors to Niagara Falls had carried away so much moisture with them. However, despite being damp and tired, all three agreed that they had enjoyed the day – the Girl in the Red Dress enthusiastically remarking, "We've had a glorious lark!"

Laura Bradshaw Durand, alias "Pharos," continued her career in journalism until her passing on July 10, 1925.

Annie Edson Taylor: First Over the Falls in a Barrel

52

Clouds of dust whirled around the stagecoach as it raced along the road from San Antonio to Austin, Texas. It was 1872 and the stage was the only public transportation available between the two towns. On board were six men and one woman. The men were all wealthy citizens of San Antonio, while the woman had been a school teacher there for the past three years but was now returning to her former home in the northern United States. Her name was Annie Edson Taylor.

Annie Taylor poses with her barrel and her cat.

Francis J. Petrie Collection, Niagara Falls, Ontario, Public Library.

Suddenly, as the road passed through a wooded area, three masked men appeared on horseback and proceeded to hold up the stage. The men on board were soon relieved of their money. One of the robbers then approached Annie who had several hundred dollars in bills pinned in the folds of her dress. He demanded to know if she had any money. Annie responded that she had "a little."

Pressing a revolver to her temple, he told her to hand it over or "I'll blow out your brains." Annie coolly replied, "Blow away. I would as soon be without brains as without money." The robbers gave a laugh, mounted their horses and rode off. Annie had kept her money.

The story reveals two things about Annie Edson Taylor: she had considerable courage and she feared poverty more than anything else including death. It was this same fear that, years later, would cause her to again summon that courage in order to do something nobody had ever attempted: go over Niagara Falls in a barrel.

Annie Edson was born in 1838, in Cayuga County, New York, not far from the town of Auburn. Orphaned at twelve, her guardian sent her to an excellent boarding school at Charlotteville, New York, just west of Albany.

In 1856, she married David Taylor, a medical student 13 years her senior. The marriage was not a happy one. Following the outbreak of the Civil War in 1861, David joined the Union Army. Seriously wounded during June 1864, he died some months later.

Annie was now destitute. It was at this point that she vowed to do whatever was necessary, as long as it was legal and moral, to keep from being forced into the same situation again.

Ambitious and determined to make it on her own, she borrowed money from a friend and enrolled in the Normal School at Albany. She completed the four year teaching course in three, graduating with honours.

Shortly after, she headed for San Antonio where she hoped to find a teaching position and also look up a friend who had moved there. She found both the friend and the job but after three years returned to the north escaping, as we have seen, robbery and death in the process.

Heading to New York City, Annie enrolled in a school of dance. Following a great deal of hard work, she became a qualified instructor and, over the next several decades, taught dance and physical culture in a number of cities across the United States. Thanks to the generosity of several friends, she also had the opportunity to spend an extended period in Europe and Mexico.

By the summer of 1901, Annie, now 62, was living in Bay City, Michigan. Her career as a dance instructor was over and, with her savings almost gone, she was staring at poverty. There was no such thing as social security and Annie had no husband or children to help her.

She needed a moneymaking inspiration and soon. As she put it in her auto-biography, "My thought was if I could do something no one else in the world had ever done, I could make some money honestly and quickly." One night in late July she was reading a newspaper article about the Niagara frontier when the inspiration came "like a flash of light": she would go over Niagara Falls in a barrel!

Annie never had any second thoughts about the idea. She went to work immediately, drawing up plans for her barrel and then hiring a Bay City cooperage to make it. When completed, the oak barrel weighed 72 kilograms (160 pounds).

She hired a manger, Frank "Tussie" Russell, promising to pay him after her trip over the Falls when, she was confident, money would come pouring in, although just how this would happen she wasn't sure.

Annie, Frank and the barrel arrived in Niagara Falls, New York, by train on October 13, 1901. The local press described her as "agile, athletic and strong." Some reporters, however, tactfully noted that she really didn't look to be only 42, as Annie was claiming.

On October 18, a trial run was made with a cat in the barrel. While the cask survived intact, accounts differ about the feline's fate, some claiming the cat was uninjured, while others reported that it lost all of its nine lives in the plunge.

After several post-ponements due to poor weather and other problems, the trip was scheduled for Thursday, October 24 – Annie's 63rd birthday. For the first time, a human being was going to challenge mighty Niagara Falls.

The momentous voyage began with Annie and her barrel being rowed out to Grass Island, a speck of land on the American side of the Niagara River, about 1.6 kilometres (1 mile) above the Horseshoe Falls. Here she got into her barrel, which was equipped with a harness and a number of cushions for padding. An anvil provided ballast.

A dazed Annie Taylor is helped ashore after becoming the first person to go over the Falls in a barrel. It was October 24, 1901.

Niagara Falls Heritage Foundation Collection, Niagara Falls, Ontario, Public Library.

The hatch was closed and Annie was then given a supply of air using a bicycle pump attached to a valve on the barrel.

Two experienced Niagara River boatmen, Fred Truesdale and Billy Holleran, towed the cask out into the proper current. At 4:05, Annie was cut loose. Eighteen minutes later the barrel slipped over the deadly precipice and down into the seething cauldron below.

The large crowd gathered on both sides of the river waited with breathless suspense.

Suddenly, they heard the tooting of a whistle. Captain Richard Carter, piloting the *Maid of the Mist*, had spotted the barrel. After some minutes, a member of the recovery crew snagged it with a grappling hook and pulled it onto a rock not far from the Canadian *Maid of the Mist* landing. Frantically, the lid was pried off and John Ross, who worked for the *Maid of the Mist*, peered inside.

Reacting to the sudden light, Annie blinked.

"She's alive!" yelled Ross.

There was a great shout of joy as Annie extended a limp hand through the opening and waved to the crowd. When she was finally extracted from the barrel (she had to be sawed out), Annie was cold, wet (the barrel was nearly half full of water), in shock and bleeding from a gash on the right side of her head. But she had survived – achieving something no other human being had ever done. She later described the experience this way: "I felt as though all nature had been annihilated."

Unfortunately, the financial windfall she had hoped for never materialized. While she eventually presented a program about her exploit in some American cities, it was soon evident that neither her personality nor her appearance was particularly suitable for the stage.

What little money she did make from her famous plunge mostly came from selling pamphlets and autographed pictures of herself on street corners in Niagara Falls, New York.

By February 1921, Annie, penniless and nearly blind, was forced to do something she had desperately tried to avoid all her life – seek public charity. She was sent to live in the county infirmary in Lockport, New York.

It was there that she passed away on April 29, 1921. Several months before her death she had lamented to a newspaper reporter, "I did what no other woman in the world had the nerve to do only to become a pauper."

Burial took place in Oakwood Cemetery, Niagara Falls, New York.

The Pan-American Exposition: Celebrating Electricity from Niagara Falls 53

On May 1, 1901, a huge international extravaganza opened in Buffalo. Called the Pan-American Exposition, its purpose was to stimulate trade and friendship between the nations of North, Central and South America.

The biggest event of its kind ever held along the Niagara Frontier, the fair attracted some eight million visitors over its six-month run. There had been quite a rivalry between Buffalo and Niagara Falls, New York, over the right to host the Pan-American Exposition. Since the major theme of the show was to be "The New Electric Age," Niagara Falls, which had already become an important centre for hydro electric generation, felt it should get the nod. In the end, however, Buffalo, with its much larger population and excellent railroad network, was chosen.

The legend of the Maid of the Mist was used as the motif for the official poster of the Pan-American Exposition held in Buffalo in 1901. Designed by Evelyn Rumsey Cary, the poster shows the nymph in the waters of Niagara Falls.

Sherman Zavitz Collection.

The fair was held on a 140-hectare (350-acre) site stretching from Delaware Avenue west to Elmwood Avenue, and from the New York Central rail lines south

The Electric Tower was the focal point of the Pan-American Exposition.
Sherman Zavitz Collection.

to Delaware Park, a portion of which was included in the grounds.

A considerable number of elaborate buildings were constructed. Some of these were erected by participating countries such as Canada, while others were for particular themes such as horticulture, music, agriculture and, of course, electricity. Since the buildings were meant to be temporary, all but one were made out of wire, wood framing and plaster of Paris. The exception was the New York State Pavilion. It was to be permanent, so was constructed of white marble in the classical style. (Since 1902, it has been the home of the Buffalo and Erie County Historical Society.)

The exposition's most spectacular structure was the Electric Tower. One hundred and twenty metres (400 feet) high, it was illuminated at night with 11,000 eight-watt bulbs. Visitors could take an elevator to the observation deck and then continue to the cupola by means of a spiral staircase. On top of the cupola was the huge gilded figure of the Goddess of Light, while the base of the tower featured a miniature Niagara Falls, the source of Buffalo's electricity.

Not only was the Electric Tower lighted each night, but all the other many buildings were as well. With a total of 200,000 bulbs, it was a dazzling show, creating, as the local press put it, "glorious lighting effects that have never been witnessed in any part of the world."

The fair's $2,500,000 midway featured such attractions as Dreamland, A Trip to the Moon, House-Upside-Down, The Scenic Railroad, Bonner - The Educated Horse, Chiquita - The Doll Lady and a merry-go-round. Near the midway was a 12,000-seat stadium for athletic events.

There were a number of restaurants and several man-made lakes connected to a 1.6 kilometre (one mile) canal, which wound its way through the grounds.

People could ride an electric launch or hire a gondola for a lovely water trip around the site.

The exposition was immensely popular, although marred by a tragedy. This came on the afternoon of September 6. While hosting a public reception in the Temple of Music, U.S. President William McKinley was shot by a self-proclaimed anarchist. He died three days later.

On the morning of September 6, the president had visited Niagara Falls, New York, even going out onto the Falls View Bridge, which was located close to where the Rainbow Bridge is now. He stopped short of the halfway point, however, since up to that time no president had left the United States while in office.

The Pan-American Exposition had a definite effect on Niagara Falls, Ontario. For one thing, there were twice as many visitors that year. In its annual report for 1901, The Niagara Parks Commission (as it is now called) noted that in spite of the great increase in tourism that year, there had been no crime whatsoever in Queen Victoria Park. This happy state of affairs was largely due to the efforts of the Parks Police. Credit was also given to the Provincial Police who, as the report stated: "prevented the admission into Ontario of the thieves, pickpockets and confidence men who thronged the many points of contact with the American side, but who found practically no opportunity for carrying on their nefarious work on this side of the river."

In anticipation of many additional visitors, the commission had built several new and larger washroom facilities, one of which was "flushed by a constant stream of spring water."

the Temple of Music, where President William McKinley was assassinated on September 6, 1901. Sherman Zavitz Collection.

Several American businessmen, also realizing there would be a great influx of tourists to Niagara Falls during 1901, had applied to the commission for approval to erect two special attractions. One of them wished to construct a cable car ride across the gorge from Table Rock to Goat Island directly in front of the Horseshoe Falls, while the other wanted to operate a Ferris wheel in Queen Victoria Park. The commission didn't waste any time in rejecting these applications.

As a tie-in to the exposition's major theme of electricity, the Falls, as well as the Whirlpool Rapids, were illuminated each night that summer by powerful searchlights "on a scale never before attempted."

Not surprisingly, the Parks Commission played a prominent role in the exposition's horticulture show. The commission's chief gardener, Roderick Cameron, displayed a new variety of begonias that he had developed and which "attracted very much attention for its great wealth of bloom and graceful habit." His dahlias also won a number of awards.

Following the close of the fair on November 1, the buildings were taken down and the land sold for development.

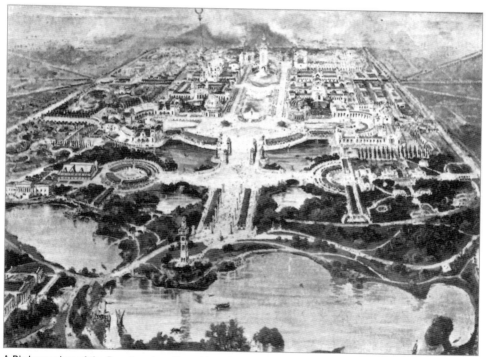

A Birdseye view of the Pan-American Exposition site in Buffalo, 1901.
Sherman Zavitz Collection.

Maud Willard:
Trapped in the Niagara River Whirlpool

In 1901, Maud Willard shot the lower rapids of the Niagara River in a barrel. She then became trapped in the Whirlpool, which resulted in deadly consequences.

Niagara Parks Archives.

The crowds gathered around the Niagara River Whirlpool watched with ever-increasing concern as hour after hour the barrel was tossed and tumbled in the grip of the vicious current.

Inside that barrel was a young woman by the name of Maud Willard whose life was obviously in great peril. Originally from Ohio, Maud had been performing at a Buffalo theatre when she agreed to do a stunt with Carlisle Graham. Back on July 11, 1886, he had been the first person to shoot the Whirlpool Rapids in a barrel. Since that day, he had repeated the trip four times.

Now it was September 7, 1901, and Graham had arranged a double performance. Maud Millard was going to go through the rapids in his barrel. He would wait for her on the American side of the Whirlpool and then swim behind the barrel as it continued downriver to Lewiston.

At 3:40 p.m., Maud, along with her pet terrier, was placed in the barrel at the *Maid of the Mist* landing and towed out into the middle of the Niagara River where she was then set adrift. At four o'clock, she rushed under the Whirlpool Rapids Bridge and five minutes later reached the Whirlpool.

As planned, Graham was waiting for her. When the barrel come into sight, he put on his life preserver. He also tied a life ring around his neck to keep his head supported should the water knock him out. Graham then waited for the barrel to be shot out of the Whirlpool and continue its downstream journey so he could begin his swim. However, after nearly an hour had gone by and the barrel was still trapped, he decided to go ahead with his part of the performance without Maud.

Graham's swim was completed without incident. After walking back to the Whirlpool, however, he was shocked to find the barrel still caught in the raging water. He hurried back to Lewiston, crossed the bridge there, and came up to the Ontario bank of the Whirlpool, thinking he might be better able to retrieve the barrel from that side.

Dusk had fallen as Graham swam out to try and bring it in. He failed.

It was several hours later before the combined efforts of two men, Captain Johnson and Archie Donald, finally captured the barrel and got it ashore. Frantically the cover was ripped off and the rescue crew peered inside. Their worst fears were confirmed. Maud Wilson was dead.

Her pet dog was alive and well, however. It had apparently survived by putting its nose into the barrel's only air hole, thereby getting air for itself but cutting off Maud's supply so that she eventually suffocated.

Carisle Graham was devastated and never again attempted a stunt through the rapids.

Around 2 a.m., a number of Maud's friends arrived at the Whirlpool to claim the body and bring it up from the water's edge. A Toronto *Globe* reporter covering the story was not impressed by what he saw: "They half carried, half dragged the body of the woman up by her feet and hair. Some were carrying burning embers and torches to light their way; others were falling off the rugged pathways in their drunken stupor as they climbed up the narrow pathway. The worst kind of blasphemy resounded through the glen at the pool and, with flying burning embers before the high wind, presented a weird sight not unlike Dante's Inferno."

It had been a dramatic and tragic day on the Niagara River.

Ed Delahanty:
A Baseball Great Dies on the Niagara | 55

Baseball great Ed Delahanty either jumped or fell from the International Railway Bridge which crosses the Niagara River between Fort Erie and Buffalo.

Sherman Zavitz Collection.

At around 8:30 on the morning of July 9, 1903, William LeBlond was working at the Canadian *Maid of the Mist* landing when he suddenly saw a gruesome sight. Floating in the water was the body of a man. It was badly bloated, partly decomposed and naked, except for a necktie, shoes and socks. As well, the stomach was torn open and the leg had been almost severed from the thigh. There was little doubt that the body had come over the Horseshoe Falls.

LeBlond notified the police who arranged for the remains to be taken to the Morse Funeral Home on Main Street in Niagara Falls, Ontario.

When news of the discovery reached the offices of the *Cataract Journal* in Niagara Falls, New York, one of its reporters had an idea about the identity of the victim. He went to view the body and felt his suspicions were confirmed when he examined the dead man's fingers. They were bent, with abnormally large joints, while the little finger of the left hand was very crooked, as though it had been broken a number of times. They were, the reporter realized, "baseball hands." He was sure the body was that of Ed Delahanty, one of the best known ball players of the day, and who had been missing since the previous July 2. Later, a younger brother of the victim, also hearing of the discovery, came from Buffalo and made a positive identification.

"Big Ed" Delahanty had enjoyed a remarkable career in baseball. Born in Cleveland in 1867, he began playing the game at a very young age. After working his way through the minors, he played for the Philadelphia Phillies of the National League and at the time of his death was with the American League Washington Senators. He became one of the game's greatest sluggers – the "King of Swat." He

145

could hit the ball so far that home runs by other players were referred to as "Delahanty bunts." Legend had it that on one occasion he had hit a ball so hard it split in two. His career batting average of .346, recorded between 1888 and 1903, is still among the best ever. He was also one of the first players to hit four home runs in a single game.

"Big Ed" Delahanty (1867-1903).
A legendary baseball player who met a mysterious end.

Sherman Zavitz Collection.

On Sunday, June 28, 1903, Delahanty and his Washington teammates arrived in Detroit for a series with the Tigers. For some weeks Ed's behaviour had been very irrational. Often his hands trembled and he raved incoherently. At other times he seemed to be hallucinating. Once he threatened to kill himself, and another time chased a fellow player with a large knife. To complicate matters, he was drinking heavily. Sometime during the afternoon of July 2, Delahanty left his Detroit hotel and completely vanished.

After his body was discovered at Niagara Falls seven days later, the pieces of the puzzle quickly came together. It was learned that on the day of his disappearance he had boarded a Michigan Central train bound for New York. (The Michigan Central line ran from Detroit to Buffalo by way of southern Ontario between Windsor and Fort Erie.)

Delahanty's behaviour on the train was drunk and disorderly. At one point he attempted to pull a lady passenger out of a berth by her ankles. Conductor John Cole and the other passengers had all had enough, and when they reached Fort Erie, at 10:45 p.m., Cole gently forced him off the train. It then moved on across the International Railway Bridge over the Niagara River and into Buffalo.

Sam Kingston, night guard on the bridge, watched the train go by and then a few minutes later began his patrol. He was almost to the centre of the bridge when he suddenly saw a man standing alongside the tracks. When Kingston demanded to know what he was doing, the stranger threatened to "break his face." As the guard made a move toward him, the man ran off into the darkness towards the Buffalo end of the span. A moment later, in the distance, Kingston heard a splash followed by a cry for help. But Ed Delahanty was beyond help now and nobody would ever know if he accidentally fell or deliberately jumped into the fast-flowing Niagara River.

His body was sent to Cleveland for burial.

In 1945 Delahanty was elected to the Baseball Hall of Fame in Cooperstown, New York. He is one player, however, remembered not only for his accomplishments, but because of his mysterious death at Niagara.

Along with electricity, it is probably the best known product identified with Niagara Falls: Shredded Wheat.

This famous breakfast cereal was developed by Henry Perky, a visionary who combined shrewd business sense with a flair for showmanship.

Raised in Ohio, Perky was involved in a number of careers, including manufacturing, teaching and law. Moving to Nebraska, he entered politics, becoming a state senator at the age of twenty-five.

In 1879, poor health took him to what he hoped would be the restorative mountain air of Colorado. There he built the Denver Central Railroad and manufactured the world's first steel passenger rail cars. However, his success in business was not matched by any improvement in his health.

While studying nutrition in the hope of curing his stomach problems, Perky came up with the idea of boiling whole, unground wheat. Eating this seemed to help him and he spent the next number of years refining the product to make it easier to prepare and more palatable.

Shredded Wheat was manufactured in Niagara Falls beginning in 1904. This advertising card from the 1930s shows a painting of the Falls as well as the Canadian plant. At onetime, both were featured on the Shredded Wheat box.

Sherman Zavitz Collection.

His work resulted in the development of a machine that would cut the cooked and softened kernels of wheat into shreds. These were then formed into biscuits and baked. The result was a tasty and nutritious cereal. It was officially launched in a Denver cracker bakery in 1893. The first plant devoted solely to the making of Shredded Wheat (as Perky named his new product) was opened in Worcester, Massachusetts, two years later.

Convinced that poor nutrition lay at the root of society's ills and that Shredded Wheat could cure those ills, Perky then came up with an innovative idea to get the message out about his cereal. He would build a manufacturing plant the likes of which the world had never seen.

It would be located in a city where vast throngs of people constantly congregated – people who would not only see the plant and the name Shredded Wheat, but who would also have the opportunity to look inside and see how the cereal was made.

Perky realized there was only one place for such a plant: Niagara Falls.

Accordingly, in 1901, he opened his huge model factory (or Conservatory of Natural Science, as he called it) in Niagara Falls, New York.

It was revolutionary, described at the time as "the cleanest, finest and most hygienic factory in the world." A 5,850 square-metre (65,000 square-foot) complex of glass, brick and marble, it was one of the first factories to feature what was teamed "perfect ventilation" and automatic heat control. With 844 windows or around 30,000 panes of glass, the building was dubbed "The Palace of Light."

It was an extraordinary structure as well as a masterstroke of public relations and advertising. Before long, 100,000 people a year were visiting Perky's conservatory where, following the tour, they could enjoy a complimentary bowl of Shredded Wheat.

In 1904, a branch of the American parent firm known as the Canadian Shredded Wheat Company, established a plant in Niagara Falls, Ontario. While not as large as the factory on the other side of the Niagara River, it operated under the same strict sanitary conditions.

In a profile of the local operation published by the Niagara Falls, Ontario, *Daily Record* in 1907, it was noted, "The wisdom of the company in erecting this plant has been amply justified by the wonderful growth of the Canadian business, the consumption of Shredded Wheat in Canada having increased 51 percent during the year 1906."

The article concluded with a ringing endorsement for the locally-made product: "It is the favourite breakfast food of intelligent, discriminating Canadians and is rapidly displacing the old-time porridge, which was seldom properly cooked and was always bolted down without chewing."

The Canadian plant also offered tours and a dish of Shredded Wheat for visitors.

Both plants also featured a picture of their respective building, a painting of the Falls and the words ''The Original Niagara Falls Product'' on every box of Shreaded Wheat. These promotional ideas came from Henry Perky and did much to create the famous connection between Niagara Falls and Shredded Wheat.

All the Shredded Wheat plants were bought by Nabisco (The National Biscuit Co.) in 1928. Perky's grand conservatory was taken down in 1963, by which time production of Shredded Wheat in Niagara Falls, New York had been relocated to another building. As of early 1996, the famous cereal was no longer manufactured in the American city.

The Niagara Falls, Ontario, plant is now owned by Post Foods Canada. A variety of cereals, including Shredded Wheat, continue to be made there.

H.G. Wells:
A "Frightening Vision"

57

H.G. Wells is an author synonymous with clever, entertaining and, often, terrifying stories. He was also a man who had plenty to say about Niagara Falls.

Born in England in 1866, Herbert George Wells is considered by many to be the father of modern science fiction. A number of his novels, such as *The Time Machine*, *The Island of Dr. Moreau*, *The War of the Worlds* and *The Invisible Man*, have become classics in English literature.

Wells visited Niagara Falls in 1906. His account of the visit appeared that same year in the journal *Harper's Weekly* under the depressing title *The End of Niagara*. After exploring both the Canadian and American sides of the Niagara River, Wells was decidedly blunt, writing, "Niagara's spectacular effect, its magnificent and humbling size and splendor were long since destroyed beyond recovery by the

A pivotal battle in the H.G. Wells novel *The War In the Air* takes place in the skies over Niagara Falls. This illustration by Eric Pape shows part of that conflict.

From H.G. Wells, *The War In The Air* (1908).

hotels, the factories, the powerhouses, the bridges and tramways and hoardings that arose about it." (Hoardings were similar to today's billboards.)

He almost trivializes Niagara: "One has gone behind half a hundred downpours just as impressive in Switzerland; a hundred tons of water is really just as stunning as ten million."

There were, however, some positive notes in an otherwise negative narrative. Although he felt the Falls seen from the Canadian side "have a peculiar long majesty of effect," an even grander view was the "sea-wide" Niagara River just upstream from the Falls. This was like a "limitless ocean" that "gripped the imagination as nothing else there seemed to do."

Still, Wells was more interested in the human involvement around the Falls than nature's creations. Much of the human effort and accomplishment here he found to be "defiling and ugly." But to a certain degree he excused these as earlier examples of what he called the "human-growth process."

What excited Wells the most during his visit were the power plants – not the buildings themselves, but what was inside them. Impressed by technological progress, he was in the right place at the right time since in 1906 Niagara Falls was in the forefront of generating electricity using waterpower. Entering one of the plants, he described its turbines as "noble masses of machinery." He approved of the idea of using Niagara's water this way. In fact, it was "altogether well" that Niagara would soon come to an end if its waters "should rise again in light and power."

Wells saw the electrical generation at Niagara as a prime example of the long human struggle to master nature. He felt that humans had almost won the contest and was pleased about that. But he had some concerns about what sort of world would result from the victory.

Two years after his visit here Wells wrote a science fiction novel in which Niagara Falls has a prominent role. Entitled *The War in the Air*, this gloomy story describes how technological advances, particularly the air ship, nearly destroy humanity instead of helping it.

Most of the world's major nations have built large air fleets, with Germany creating the most powerful. That country's leader, Prince Karl Albert, orders his fleet across the Atlantic to attack the United States. After wiping out New York City, the Germans come to Niagara where the prince wants to build a fortress so he can take advantage of the "enormous power works." Everyone living in a large radius around the Falls is forced away and all the buildings are bombed as the Germans consolidate their position here.

Japan and China then join forces to build a massive air fleet. It crosses the Pacific and advances on Niagara where the Asians and the Germans engage in a terrible fight in the skies over the Falls. As the Asians get the upper hand, the German flagship is shot down in the upper rapids and plunges over the cataracts.

The victors take the conflict to the rest of North America and then to Europe. Soon the entire world is engulfed in war both in the air and on the ground where there are riots and revolts. The whole fabric of civilization begins to melt away. This was a frightening vision of the future and Niagara's role in that future as H.G. Wells' vivid imagination saw it back in 1908.

Oscar Williams: The "Slide for Life"

58

City Hall, Niagara Falls, Canada.

Oscar Williams, one of Niagara's many "stunters," performed a rewarding feat at the Niagara Falls, Ontario City Hall flagpole in 1911.

John Burtniak Colleciton.

People went white with fear. Many fainted, while others shrieked or were too paralysed to make any sound at all.

The reason for these reactions was a man hanging from a wire 52 metres (170 feet) above the centre of the Niagara Gorge and unable to move forward or backward. A stunt had gone wrong.

It was June 14, 1910, and an International Carnival was taking place at Niagara. One of the carnival's highlights was to be a "Slide for Life", performed by Oscar Williams of Niagara Falls, New York who often billed himself as "The Great Houdin." Williams, a painter and steeplejack by trade, was going to slide on a wire stretched nearly 450 metres (1,500 feet) across the Niagara River Gorge while hanging by his teeth from a pulley.

Thousands of people had gathered on both sides of the river to witness this daring and unusual stunt. At exactly 5:30 p.m., Williams started out from the American side. His wire extended across the gorge just below the Upper Steel Arch Bridge, near the site of today's Rainbow Bridge.

Only a few metres out, the pulley apparatus began to stick and Williams had to thrash his body about to keep it going. After about 90 metres (300 feet) had been covered, he picked up speed and rushed past the middle point of the wire where, however, a considerable sag now developed. As a result, when the pulley reached the steep upgrade, headed for the Canadian side, there was not enough momentum, causing it to slow down, stop, and then roll backwards, coming to rest in the slack of the wire. The Niagara Falls *Review* described him as "a poor little speck of humanity hanging directly over the centre of the river."

Fortunately, he had taken a rope saddle with him and, after putting it in place, was able to sit and no longer hang by his teeth from the pulley. However, all the movement on the slender wire had caused it to swing dangerously and many in the huge crowd were sure it would snap, throwing Williams into the river far below.

The stunter tried everything he could think of to get to the Canadian side, but nothing worked. He was marooned.

Firemen from Niagara Falls, New York, were summoned and began a sensational rescue attempt. They set a pulley on Williams' wire to which were attached two ropes. One was a guide rope to work the pulley out to him, and the other was let down to the river and the *Maid of the Mist*, which had moved into position directly under Williams. Captain Carter grabbed the end of this rope and hung on. When the pulley, guided by firemen from the Upper Steel Arch Bridge, reached the stunter, he worked his way out of the saddle and began his descent, finally landing on the steamer's deck. The Niagara Falls *Gazette* noted: "As he did so the little vessel set up a great tooting of its whistle and the crowds sent up a

Oscar Williams, "The Great Houdin" extended the wire for his "Slide for Life" just below the Upper Steel Arch Bridge, popularly known as the Honeymoon Bridge.

John Burtniak Colleciton.

great cheer." Oscar Williams had given his audience a thrill and a scare they would never forget.

A year and a day later, Williams made a rescue of sorts himself in Niagara Falls, Ontario. While walking about looking for work, he passed the city hall on Queen Street. (It was the building, greatly altered, that still stands in front of the present city hall.) Here he noticed Charles Baldwin, who was in charge of the grounds, staring in frustration at the top of the 29-metre (96-foot)-high flag pole where the Union Jack had become entangled around an iron beaver ornament. For a dollar Williams offered to climb up and rescue the flag. Baldwin told him to go ahead.

While keeping a firm grasp on the pole with his left hand, he used his right to alternately tie two ropes as stirrups, and so gradually made his way to the top where he worked the flag free. Baldwin and Mayor Dores, who had come out of his city hall office to watch, were so impressed by the feat that, as soon as the stunter and steeplejack was back on the ground, they promptly doubled his pay. Williams walked away with two dollars in his pocket!

"The Great Houdin" attempted another slide across the Niagara Gorge on June 28, 1911. Exactly the same problem developed as the year before and again he had to be rescued.

On July 4, 1913, Williams tried his stunt once more. This time, however, his wire was stretched between the courthouse and jail in Mayville, New York. It turned out to be his final performance. Whereas the problem on both previous occasions had been a lack of momentum to carry him all the way across the wire, this time there was far too much speed and he could not stop his pulley before it smashed into a pole at the end of the slide. His skull was crushed. Oscar Williams' "Slide for Life" became a slide to death.

Lincoln Beachey:
The "Flying Fool" at Niagara Falls

59

Lincoln Beachey's claim to Niagara stunting fame was flying under the Upper Steel Arch Bridge on June 28, 1911.

William E. Chajkowsky, *Royal Flying Corps: Borden to Texas to Beamsville* (1979).

The last week of June 1911 was a time that most residents of both Niagara Falls, Ontario, and Niagara Falls, New York, would long remember. The reason for this was a huge international carnival that featured, among many special events, the appearance of the first airplane at Niagara. It was a Curtis biplane piloted by Lincoln Beachey, an American aviator employed by the Glen Curtis Aircraft Company of Nebraska.

The 24-year-old Beachey, considered a daring and dashing pilot, came here after learning that $1,000 would be given to anyone presenting an "air show" at the carnival.

Aviation was still in its infancy at the time. It had only been eight years since the Wright brothers had made the first successful flight at Kitty Hawk, North Carolina. Canadian aviation was born with the flight of the *Silver Dart* at Baddeck, Nova Scotia, in 1909.

Beachey first flew from Nebraska to Fort Erie, landing at the racetrack there on June 26. The following day he flew to Niagara Falls, New York, by way of Buffalo. He made the flight in 16 minutes and landed in a six-hectare (15-acre) field along 27th Street, a spot he had previously selected. Around 12,000 people cheered as he stepped from his craft and was welcomed by Mayor P. J. Keller.

June 28 had been chosen as the day for Beachey's performance, and the huge crowds that gathered that afternoon on both sides of the river were not disappointed. As the Niagara Falls, Ontario, *Daily Record* wrote, "After waiting patiently all afternoon for the appearance of the birdman, the crowds in the parks and the thoroughfares were at last rewarded when at 5:40 p.m. Beachey rose into the air from the American side. Rising rapidly, the aviator passed over the upper rapids against the wind, turned when opposite the Canadian Niagara Power Plant and came back over the Horseshoe Falls and Upper Steel Arch Bridge." (The Upper Steel Arch Bridge was located close to where the Rainbow Bridge is today.)

After repeating the routine, he flew over Queen Victoria Park and then out over the river again. Now came the climax of the show. As the *Daily Record* reported, "Turning quickly, Beachey came swiftly downwards and gracefully and easily passed under the arches of the bridge." The vast crowd went wild. Not only had most never seen an airplane before, but to see one flying over the Falls for the first time as well as perform a "stunt" by going under the bridge all added up to an exciting and memorable spectacle. A great shout went up from the spectators while "words of wonder at the most daring feat ever performed were heard on every side."

Beachey flew on down over the gorge until he was almost at the Whirlpool Rapids Bridge. He then turned westward towards the Canadian side and, after circling twice over Epworth Circle, landed in an open area near Victoria Avenue. The next day he flew over the gorge several times and went downriver as far as Queenston before returning to Niagara Falls, Ontario. He then collected his $1,000 and took off for Toronto.

Speaking to a Toronto reporter that evening, he frankly admitted, "I would not again attempt to fly under that bridge for five thousand dollars, let alone for the thousand dollar purse that I won today. It is the uncertainty as to what is before the aviator as he passes through the clouds of spray over the falls that makes the flight so perilous. As I passed through the spray and out into the daylight again, I dipped my machine and made directly for the bridge. I was within a few hundred feet of the bridge before I was sure that my attempt to pass under it would be successfully accomplished."

Lincoln Beachey, who was often referred to as the "flying fool," went on to thrill audiences with his aviation expertise until he was killed during an air show over San Francisco in 1915.

February 4, 1912: Tragedy on the Ice

60

Sunday, February 4, 1912, was a clear, windy and very cold day in Niagara Falls. Nevertheless, hundreds of people both residents and tourists were on hand that morning to view the gorgeous winter scenery around the Falls and to take a walk on the ice bridge. The happy and excited crowd had no inkling that a tragedy was about to unfold.

The ice bridge is one of Niagara's most spectacular creations. A mixture of ice and slush that has flowed down from Lake Erie drops over the Falls and when it reaches the *Maid of the Mist* eddy, just past the American Falls, it is forced into the Canadian side and jams there. As more and more ice and slush push against it, the whole mass begins to heave and hump from the continuing pressure. When the ice particles are pushed up out of the water, they freeze in an agglomerate mass, which grows to a considerable size. This "suspended glacier" eventually reaches the other side of the gorge, creating a true ice bridge.

Burrell Hecock, a Niagara Falls Hero.
James C. Morden, *Falls View Bridges and Niagara Ice Bridges* (1938).

Beginning in the 1880s, the ice bridge became a popular winter playground. Local businessmen even set up concession shanties out on the ice where one could buy drinks (including whisky), hot dogs, souvenirs and get a tintype picture taken.

Among the visitors to Niagara Falls on that fateful Sunday in 1912, were Eldridge and Clara Stanton of Toronto. The 36-year-old Eldridge acted as secretary-treasurer for his brother's printing firm. After leaving their Niagara Falls, New York, hotel around mid-morning, Eldridge and Clara, 28, took an elevator into the gorge and began exploring the hills and valleys of the ice bridge, which was estimated to be around 300 metres (1,000 feet) long and 18 metres (60 feet) thick.

As noon approached, the crowd began to thin, as people headed indoors to get warm and have some lunch. Only the Stantons and a handful of other visitors were left on the ice. Included in this small group were Ignatius Roth and

The ice bridge with the American Falls in the background just before the fatal disaster of February 4, 1912.

Francis J. Petrie Collection, Niagara Falls, Ontario, Public Library.

Burrell Hecock. Natives of Cleveland, both were 17 years old and had been life-long friends. Also still on the ice was William "Red" Hill Sr., the well-known riverman from Niagara Falls, Ontario.

Suddenly, a few minutes before noon, a loud ominous crack like the lash of a whip was heard. Seconds later the ice bridge began to break up and move downstream. Hill yelled a warning and ran for the Canadian shore. Most of the others also reacted quickly and made it safely to either the Canadian or American side. However, the Stantons, Roth and Hecock, standing on a huge, moving ice floe in mid-river, hesitated, not sure which way to go.

The two youths then made a dash for the Canadian shore. The Stantons went in the opposite direction, only to find their escape cut off by a wide channel. Hill, at great peril to his own safety, rushed back out onto the moving ice and yelled at the couple to head for the Canadian side. With the riverman helping them, the Stantons made it to within 15 metres (50 feet) of the riverbank when they suddenly encountered another slush-filled channel. Paralyzed with fear, Clara and Eldridge would not go on, even though Hill told them the gap could be crossed. Instead, they turned back with Hecock and Roth following. Hill now had no choice but to leave them and scramble ashore.

By now, the large floe carrying the marooned quartet was passing under the Upper Steel Arch Bridge, which stood close to where the Rainbow Bridge is now. Officials at the bridge phoned the police and fire departments, which raced to the scene.

Roth and Hecock ran on ahead of the Stantons, who were now exhausted from the exertion and tension. Clara soon collapsed, telling her husband that she couldn't go on and was ready to die there. Not able to get her up, Eldridge shouted to the two youths for help. Hecock responded, leaving Roth and going back to help get Clara on her feet.

Roth kept moving and managed to get a little closer to the Canadian shore. Red Hill, who was running along the riverbank, felt there was a chance Roth could be saved and began to shout instructions to him. The young man jumped over openings where and when he was told and struggled over the hummocks of ice. When he was close enough, Hill threw him a rope and pulled him ashore slightly over 1.6 kilometres (a mile) below the Horseshoe Falls. Roth had cheated death.

Meanwhile, the ice floe carrying the three remaining helpless victims was racing down the river and would soon be in the grip of the Whirlpool Rapids, one of the most violent stretches of white water in the world. Their last chance at rescue would be the ropes that had been lowered by the police and firemen from the Cantilever Bridge and the adjacent Whirlpool Rapids Bridge.

Just before reaching the bridges, the large floe broke into two sections, leaving the Stantons on one piece and Hecock on the other. It was Hecock who reached one of the ropes first. He grabbed it and grimly hung on. As the men on the bridge began to haul him up, the young man tried to help himself by climbing

Eldridge and Clara Stanton (inside added circle), their arms clasped around each other, ride to their deaths on an ice floe in the Whirlpool Rapids, February 4, 1912.

From George A. Seibel, *Ontario's Niagara Parks: 100 Years* (1985).

hand-over-hand. Frozen fingers and exhaustion conspired against him. As he began to lose his grip, he tried to get his legs around the rope. When this failed, he made a desperate but futile attempt to hang on with his teeth. With the rope now spinning like a top from the wind, Hecock's head fell back, he let go and plunged into the river. He was seen for a few seconds and then vanished forever.

Moments later, the Stanton's floe reached the Cantilever Bridge. Eldridge seized a rope and tried to tie it around Clara's waist. The ice was moving too fast, however, and he had to let go of the rope before he had time to tie a knot. The same thing happened with the rope hanging from the Whirlpool Rapids Bridge.

There was no hope now. An eyewitness reporter described the final moments of the drama: "He raised the woman to her feet, kissed her and clasped her in his arms. The woman then sank to her knees. The man knelt beside her; his arms clasped close about her. So they went to their death. The ice held intact until it struck the great wave. There it was shattered; there the gallant man and the woman at his side disappeared from view."

Their bodies were never found.

Burrell Hecock (inside added circle) stranded on an ice floe in the Niagara River.
Niagara Falls Heritage Foundation Collection, Niagara Falls, Ontario, Public Library.

The Great Gorge Garbage Blast

61

An unfortunate accident befell one of the open summer cars on the Great Gorge Railway in July 1913. John Burtniak Collection.

The Great Gorge Route Belt Line was one of the most spectacular and popular attractions ever available at Niagara Falls. Beginning in 1902 this electric railway line, which used open-sided trolley cars for summer travel, could offer a magnificent trip.

Boarding, for example, at Table Rock, you could then travel north through Queen Victoria Park, along River Road, past the Canadian end of the Whirlpool Rapids Bridge, and continue along the top edge of the gorge to Queenston Heights Park.

From here passengers descended by a series of sharp turns and steep grades to the Queenston-Lewiston Suspension Bridge and crossed the Niagara River. Once on the American side, the cars travelled south through the gorge right beside the river, giving them a breathtaking view of the Whirlpool and Lower Rapids.

As the railway approached the Falls, it began a long-graded rise on the side of the gorge wall until it reached Niagara Falls, New York. You could then ride across the Upper Steel Arch Bridge (near today's Rainbow Bridge) back to Canada. Of course the whole trip could be done in the opposite direction as well.

Competition from the automobile brought an end to the Canadian side of the Great Gorge Route operation in 1932. The U.S. section shut down three years later after a rock slide in the gorge destroyed a large portion of the track.

A most unusual accident, and certainly a very smelly one, occurred along the American side of the line on Sunday, July 13, 1913. In those days Niagara Falls, New York, dumped most of its garbage straight into the Niagara River by means of a large, covered chute that ran from the upper bank, down the side of the gorge and under the railway to the river. Alongside the tracks was a large opening in the chute.

At around 2:30 p.m. that day, city officials set off a stick of dynamite which had been placed in the chute to dislodge a huge clog of garbage that had developed. At the precise moment of the blast, a Great Gorge car passed by the hole in the chute. The force of the explosion moved the garbage so violently that tons of it shot out of the opening and landed all over the passengers in the open-sided car.

As quickly as possible the "victims" were brought into Niagara Falls, New York, where they ran for their hotels to clean up. The Niagara Falls, New York *Gazette* described the scene as "a horrible mess," and noted how one passenger, a Mrs. Breithaust of Kitchener, Ontario, "arrived at her room in the Tower Hotel with a full-sized banana skin clinging fondly to her hair."

When they had boarded the Great Gorge Route trolley car earlier that afternoon, those Niagara tourists were no doubt looking forward to having an unique experience – and they certainly got one!

Passengers on the Great Gorge Route were treated to a spectacular and memorable ride along the Niagara River Gorge. This view is from around 1915.

Sherman Zavitz Collection.

The Whirlpool Aero Car: Providing a View from Above

62

Flags are flying for the inaugural ride of the Spanish Aero Car (now known as the Whirlpool Aero Car) on August 8, 1916.

Sherman Zavitz Collection.

The Whirlpool Aero Car (originally called the Spanish Aero Car) is one of Niagara's most unique and popular attractions. Since 1916, millions of people have been treated to a bird's-eye view of the mighty Whirlpool as they glided across six cables some 76 metres (250 feet) above this watery spectacle.

The Niagara Spanish Aero Car Company, made up of a group of Spanish businessmen, developed the idea of a cable car ride across the Niagara River Whirlpool in 1913. Work began the following year after the company's proposal was accepted by The Niagara Parks Commission.

The system was designed, and its construction supervised, by the brilliant Spanish engineer Leonardo Torres-Quevedo. Born in 1852, he began his professional career by overseeing the construction of railway lines in southern Spain. Independently wealthy and a world traveller, Torres-Quevedo did pioneer work in calculators, computers and robots, as well as developing an improved dirigible system. He died in Madrid in 1936.

The cable car system he built to cross the Niagara River Whirlpool was the first of its kind anywhere in the world. The carriage rides on six lock coil track cables, the tensions of which are independent of the weight of the car due to counterweights at the end of each cable. Consequently, if one cable breaks, there is no danger, since there is no increase in the load carried by the other cables.

Built at a cost of $120,000, the system was installed between Colt's Point on the south side of the Whirlpool and Thompson Point on the north side – both in Ontario. These locations were named after early property owners in the area. At first, passengers could get on and off at either side. Now, Colt's Point has the only entrance and exit station. It is claimed by some that one reason this change was made was to foil scam artists. Apparently, the plan went something like this: Individuals were located in Canada who wanted to enter the United States illegally. They were told that, for a certain fee, this could be arranged using the Spanish Aero Car. The victims were then placed on board the cable car at Colt's Point and told that when it reached the "American" side they should jump off and run. This they did, not realizing, of course, that they were actually still in Canada. Obviously, the perpetrators of this scheme had to be sure their victims had no understanding of the Whirlpool's geography.

The Spanish Aero Car officially opened on August 8, 1916. Several hundred invited guests were on hand for what the Niagara Falls, Ontario, *Review* called "a splendid event." The paper provided the following details: "Shortly after 3 o'clock Mrs. J. Enoch Thompson, wife of the Spanish Consul at Toronto, opened the cable way by breaking a bottle of champagne over the gate next to the landing at Thompson Point, at which place the ceremony took place. Enthusiastic cheers followed the christening of the car."

All the guests were then given an opportunity to have a ride. The *Review* noted: "Back and forth the car went, giving the occupants their first view of the Whirlpool from above. It was a pleasing sight to watch the car, which carried four flags – the Union Jack, the Stars and Stripes, the French flag and the Spanish flag – crossing and recrossing high above the water."

Leonardo Torres-Quevedo was not present for the opening ceremonies but was undoubtedly pleased to learn of the delighted reaction to his cable car.

Operated over the years by various private interests, the Spanish Aero Car has been owned and operated by The Niagara Parks Commission since 1969. It was completely renovated and upgraded following the end of the 1984 season. Boasting a perfect safety record, the Whirlpool Aero Car continues to delight Niagara's visitors.

Two Men on a Scow: A Thrilling Rescue

63

Gustov Lofberg and James Harris (inside added circle) marooned on the scow.
Niagara Falls, Ontario, Public Library.

The rusty old scow stuck on the rocks not far upriver from the brink of the Horseshoe Falls is a mute reminder of one of Niagara's most exciting rescue episodes.

The story began around 3 p.m. on August 6, 1918, while crews from the Great Lakes Dredge and Dock Company were deepening the Niagara Falls Power Company's intake canal on the American side of the river, about 1.6 kilometres (a mile) above the Falls. Large scows, towed by tugs, were being used to take the excavated material out into the river where it was dumped.

Suddenly, one of the tugs struck a sandbar with such force that the towline snapped, allowing the scow the tug had been pulling to quickly drift into midstream and head towards the Horseshoe Falls.

On board the scow were Gustav Lofberg, 51, and 53-year-old James Harris. Lofberg was a bachelor, while Harris was married and the father of five. Despite the almost paralyzing fear that must have gripped the two men, they had the presence of mind to open the bottom dumping doors, flooding the scow's compartments. This slowed its progress until it grounded on some rocks opposite the Toronto Powerhouse.

While for the time being at least, Lofberg and Harris were not about to go over the Falls, now they were marooned in the heart of the torturous and deadly upper rapids, about 255 metres (850 feet) from the Canadian shore and approximately 792 metres (half a mile) from the brink of the cataract.

Word of the stranded men quickly spread throughout the area and great crowds soon gathered along both banks of the river.

Several Toronto Powerhouse employees had witnessed the accident and called the Niagara Falls, Ontario, fire department. Chief Al Newman and his men rushed to the scene, bringing with them a small lifesaving gun. It was carried to the roof of the generating plant and discharged. As the Niagara Falls *Review* noted, "The rope whirled toward the watching men on the scow. It spun out an estimated 300 feet and fell into the river." A second attempt brought the same result. The rope was just too short to reach the scow.

The U.S. Coast Guard at Youngstown, New York, was contacted and arrived shortly after with their larger lifeline cannon. This was more successful. When the line was shot from the roof of the powerhouse, it easily reached the scow, prompting a mighty cheer from the large number of spectators.

James Harris being rescued by a breeches buoy.
Niagara Falls, Ontario, Public Library.

Harris and Lofberg immediately tied this light rope to a crude windlass they had laboriously constructed. The Coast Guard team, under the command of Captain A. Nelson, then tied a heavier, 2.5-centimetre (1-inch)-thick rope to the lifeline, as well as a block and tackle holding a double guy line. While dozens of men on the powerhouse roof held the lines taut the stranded men began to turn their windlass. It was a difficult and slow job. "In the early evening," the *Review* reported, "after hours of torturing progress with the windlass, Lofberg and Harris reached their hands into the water to grasp the heavy rope."

As darkness fell, powerful searchlights were put up on the shore and on the powerhouse roof, eerily illuminating the site.

About 9:30, a breeches buoy (a canvas sling suspended from a pulley) was put in place on the heavy rope. Working the guy lines, the crew on the powerhouse roof began to slowly move the breeches buoy out to Lofberg and Harris.

It looked as though the two men would soon be safely back on land. But it was not to be. Part way out, the breeches buoy suddenly stopped, sending a groan of despair rippling through the crowd. It was soon determined that the line had fouled. For two hours, attempts were made to correct the problem by pulling back and forth on the guy lines, all to no avail. While it would not advance fortunately the breeches buoy could be brought back to the powerhouse.

It was now around midnight and Captain Nelson decided to temporarily suspend the rescue operation to allow him time to come up with a solution to the breeches buoy problem. This information was conveyed to the stranded men by means of a large sign illuminated by one of the lights.

Lofberg and Harris rested fitfully, wondering if at any moment the violent water racing past their scow would dislodge it and send them to their doom.

Back on shore, William "Red" Hill Sr. introduced himself to Nelson and told him that he would be willing to go out to try and correct the problem on the lines. Hill, from Niagara Falls, Ontario, was Niagara's most knowledgeable riverman and a recognized hero who had recently returned home after having been wounded and gassed in France while serving in the First World War. Hill was told that the line was presumed safe, although it had not been tested under a weight. He replied that he was willing to take the risk.

Shortly after three o'clock in the morning, Hill went out in the breeches buoy. With the beam from a searchlight following him, he reached the trouble spot and untangled the lines. Problems continued, however, and at 5:30 Hill had to make a second trip out on the lines.

Finally, all difficulties were overcome and the breeches buoy reached the marooned men. Harris was first off the scow, reaching the powerhouse roof at 8:50 a.m., after being slowly pulled to safety across the turbulent water. Lofberg arrived about an hour later. With each arrival, a great cheer went up from the crowd.

A doctor examined both men but, although weak from hunger and fatigue, they were remarkably fit considering their 19-hour ordeal. Harris later told reporters that he was going to tie himself to a tree well inland so, as he put it, "I'll know I'm safe." The following morning, after a solid night's sleep, the two men were back at work.

A salvage operation to recover the scow was not considered feasible, and so, although some deterioration has taken place, the scow still clings to its rocky perch.

Charles Stephens: The Bristol Barber Challenges Niagara | 64

Charles Stephens poses from inside his barrel. He went over the Falls on July 11, 1920.
From Francis J. Petrie, *Roll Out the Barrel* (1985).

Charles Stephens was a man who relished living on the edge.

A barber by profession in Bristol, England, he supplemented his income by performing as a "tempter of fate," as he put it, under the name 'Professor Stephens'. He once kissed a lion and put his head in its mouth while tickling the big cat. On another occasion, he shaved a man while in a lion's cage.

In British music halls, professional knife-throwers tossed their blades to within a hair's width of his body and sharpshooters blasted sugar cubes off the top of his head. Stephens also became well known for performing parachute drops and jumping off bridges.

He was born in Bristol in 1862. As a young man, he had several close escapes from death, leading him to believe that he must have a charmed life. He also realized that in what for most people would be frightening situations, he had the ability to completely erase fear from his mind. As a result, he became a part-time showman, performing death-defying acts.

He volunteered for service in the First World War and became a decorated hero. Following the war, he resumed his barbering career in Bristol, were he was known as the barber who could wield the fastest straight razor in town.

Stephens freely admitted that he moonlighted as a daredevil performer strictly for the money. While his exploits had earned him some financial reward, by 1920, he became convinced that his biggest payoff would come from going over Niagara Falls in a barrel. At that point, only two other persons, Annie Edson Taylor and Bobby Leach, had made such a trip. Both had survived and Stephens was absolutely convinced he would as well.

Charles Stephens' barrel at the start of his trip over the Horseshoe Falls.
Niagara Falls, Ontario, Public Library.

Accordingly, he went ahead with plans to have a special barrel constructed in London, England. Made of 5-centimetre (2-inch)-thick Russian white oak, it was slightly over 1.8 metres (6 feet) high and weighed 270 kilograms (600 pounds).

Family and friends urged him to give up his plan, but Stephens, a father of eleven, was supremely confident. On June 17, 1920, the Bristol barber left home with his barrel and headed for Canada.

After arriving in Toronto, he made arrangements with the Canadian Aero Film Company to record his stunt. Once back in England, the plan was to not only charge people for viewing the movie, but to lecture and display his barrel in the music halls.

He reached Niagara Falls on July 6. The following day, the Niagara Falls, Ontario, *Review* noted how the stunter "visited points on both sides of the river where he might start his trip."

Several years before, Stephens had written to R.F. Carter, former captain of the *Maid of the Mist*, telling him what he hoped to do and asking for information about the Falls. The captain tried to discourage him. As soon as he got to Niagara Falls, however, Stephens looked up Captain Carter and asked him to manage his stunt. Carter refused, saying that he "did not want to be party to a suicide."

After examining Stephens' barrel, Bobby Leach told him it wasn't strong enough to survive a trip over the Falls. In particular, he felt that the iron hoops encircling the barrel were too light.

The 58-year-old Stephens remained undaunted, however, although he was concerned that authorities would try to prevent him from making the stunt. Final arrangements, therefore, were known only to his crew and a few selected others. This meant that just a handful of people were on hand for the launch, which was scheduled for 6:30 a.m., Sunday, July 11, from a site along the Niagara River about 2.4 kilometres (1.5 miles) above Chippawa.

Stephens was relaxed and confident. His barrel had been painted in black and white stripes to make it easier for the movie camera to see. The interior was well padded and had a portable light, along with an oxygen tank that contained a three-hour supply. A 45-kilogram (100-pound) anvil was at the bottom for ballast. Stephens planned to tie his feet to it. After talking with those present, including a *Review* reporter, and posing for pictures, the daredevil climbed inside the barrel and got into his harness. The lid was screwed on tightly and the barrel was towed out into the Niagara River. It was 8:05 a.m.

Only 91 metres (100 yards) out there was an ominous incident. One of the barrel's hoops broke and was seen by those on the riverbank to fall off into the water. A crew member in the motorboat that was towing Stephens made a quick examination of the barrel and then, apparently satisfied that there was no serious problem, went on with the trip.

After reaching Chippawa, the towline was cut and, as the *Review* wrote, "The barrel drifted off alone, now head forward, now feet forward, as the river currents caught it." Stephens dropped over the brink of the Horseshoe Falls at 8:50 and disappeared into the mist.

Those stationed below the Falls to watch for the barrel waited tensely as the minutes ticked by and there was no sign of it. By now, news of the stunt had flashed through Niagara Falls and a large crowd was gathered along the riverbank.

Around noon, a spectator at the *Maid of the Mist* landing noticed one of the barrel's staves floating towards shore. It was obvious that a tragedy had taken place.

The next day Stephens' right arm was discovered in the river. As the *Review* reported, "The arm had been pulled out at the shoulder and, while in good condition, showed the effects of having been pulled out by violence."

A few other pieces of the barrel were recovered but no other part of Stephens' body was ever found. It is generally believed that after going over the Falls the barrel hit the surface of the

Retrieving a stave from Charles Stephens' barrel following his fatal trip over the Falls.

Niagara Falls Heritage Foundation Collection, Niagara Falls, Ontario, Public Library.

river with such force that the anvil shot through the bottom taking Stephens with it, leaving only his right arm in the harness.

The arm was buried in an unmarked grave in a local cemetery.

Charles Stephens had been a "tempter of fate" once too often.

The Sir Adam Beck Generating Plants: Monumental Construction Projects

65

The Sir Adam Beck Generating Stations (No. 1 is on the right) as seen from the air. A portion of the huge reservoir is also visible.

Niagara Parks Archives.

A very important aspect of Niagara's heritage for over 100 years now has been the use of Niagara River water to generate electricity.

The first power plant on the Ontario side of the river was erected in 1892 and was located just above the Horseshoe Falls. It was primarily used to provide power for an electric railway line that ran alongside the Niagara River Gorge. The line ended operations in 1932.

During the first decade of the 20th century, three other generating stations were constructed in the vicinity of the Horseshoe Falls. Known as the Toronto Power Plant, the Ontario Power Generating Station and the Canadian Niagara Power Plant, these stations are no long in business, although the buildings remain.

Today it is the Sir Adam Beck Generating Stations downriver at Queenston that create the most interest. These power plants are among the most monumental construction projects ever undertaken in Ontario. Both were also extraordinary engineering achievements.

Adam Beck, from London, Ontario, became a member of the provincial legislature in 1902. Four years later he was responsible for introducing a bill in the legislature that created the Hydro-Electric Power Commission of Ontario, later known as Ontario Hydro and now Ontario Power Generation.

A publicly-owned company, Beck became the commission's first chairman, a position he held until his death in 1925.

Beck was the chief promoter of what was first called the Queenston-Chippawa Power Development. (In 1950, this power plant was renamed the Sir Adam Beck Generation Station No. 1).

Plans for the development were approved by the Ontario Legislature in January 1917. At the time, it was stated that this project "would eclipse any electric power plant previously built in the Niagara Falls area and would be larger than any even contemplated anywhere in the world."

This statement was no exaggeration.

Work on the gigantic undertaking began in May 1917. The idea was to utilize almost the entire 99-metre (326-foot) fall of the Niagara River. Chippawa Creek, which emptied into the Niagara River, was dredged and widened from its mouth at Chippawa to Montrose, a distance of slightly more than 6.4 kilometres (4 miles). This reversed the direction of the creek, allowing Niagara River water to flow into Chippawa Creek. From Montrose, an 13-kilometre (8-mile) canal (now called the Hydro Canal) was excavated to a point just south of Queenston Heights Park. Here, a large forebay was built close to the edge of the gorge. The water was then channeled into huge penstocks and allowed to drop 89 metres (295 feet) down the side of the gorge wall to the powerhouse, which was constructed alongside the Niagara River.

At one point, 8,100 people were at work on the project, which eventually cost $63 million.

The plant was opened on December 28, 1921. Beck, his daughter Marion, and Ontario Premier Ernest Charles Drury were present. At that point, only two generators had been installed. Not until 1930 did the operation reach its current size of 10 generators. Today, a small commemorative sign sits beside the generator where the opening ceremony took place back in 1921.

Work on the Beck No. 2 plant began in 1950. The powerhouse was constructed right beside the Sir Adam Beck No. 1 plant. This time, instead of digging another open-cut canal, water was brought from above the Falls by two parallel tunnels, each having a diameter of 13.5 metres (45 feet) . These concrete-lined tunnels are 8 kilometres (5 miles) long and pass directly under the city of Niagara Falls, often to a depth of 98 metres (328 feet). They carry 55 million litres (12 million gallons) of water a minute to the forebay of Station No. 2.

At its peak, around 7,600 people were at work on the immense job. Some 3,000 of them lived in three temporary "Hydro Cities" located at Chippawa, Queenston and the Whirlpool.

Sir Adam Beck No. 2 was officially opened on August 30, 1954, by the Duchess of Kent, Queen Elizabeth II's aunt. Three generators were then in operation. Eventually housing 16 generators, the Beck No. 2 project was completed in 1958. The total generating capacity of the two plants is just over 1,600,000 kilowatts.

The Sir Adam Beck Generating Stations are a testimony to the foresight, skill, imagination and determination of many individuals.

The Clifton Hotels: Ordeal by Fire

66

While admiring the beauty and tranquillity of Oakes Garden Theatre today, it is difficult to imagine that this same site, at the foot of Clifton Hill, has been the scene of two of the most spectacular fires in the history of Niagara Falls, Ontario.

The first Clifton Hotel, known as the Clifton House, was built at this location in 1833 by Harmanus Crysler. Within a few years it was the most prominent hotel at Niagara. A guidebook of the 1840s described it as a "large elegant, commodious, well-finished and well-furnished hotel, standing on the brow of the bank near the ferry, and commanding a splendid view of the Falls."

Around ten o'clock on the morning of June 26, 1898, an employee working at the rear of the hotel happened to

The first Clifton House Hotel (upper) was destroyed by fire on June 26, 1898, while the second Clifton Hotel (lower) burned on December 31, 1932.

April Petrie Collection.

glance up at the roof and noticed a small flame eating its way into the shingles near a chimney. He sounded the alarm. A ladder was raised to the roof and a bucket brigade began to work.

After a few minutes it was thought the fire had been extinguished, but then it was noticed that the flames had broken out in another area of the roof. It was clear that the fire had a good start in the attic. Fire companies from both sides of the Niagara River rushed to the scene, but poor water pressure and a strong wind hampered their efforts considerably. A huge crowd gathered as the whole building quickly became enveloped and the 65-year-old landmark was destroyed in a spectacular mass of flame and smoke.

The following day a reporter from the Niagara Falls, New York, *Daily Cataract* wrote: "All that remains today are grim walls of old time masonry, covered with

The first Clifton Hotel, known as the Clifton House, 1833-1898.

Niagara Falls Heritage Foundation Collection, Niagara Falls, Ontario, Public Library.

The second Clifton Hotel, 1906-1932.

Francis J. Petrie Collection, Niagara Falls, Ontario, Public Library.

a concrete grown yellow with age, charred timber, twisted irons, half burned wooden pillars and piles of debris. Where the famous old hotel, known the world over for its hospitality stood forty-eight hours ago, now stands a complete ruin."

In 1906 a new Clifton Hotel arose on the site of the old. It boasted 220 rooms, a large ballroom and a variety of stores. Soon it became, like its namesake predecessor, the premier summer hotel at Niagara.

However, an ironic twist of fate was waiting in the wings.

In the cold, early morning of Saturday, December 31, 1932, the hotel's winter caretaker, James Jones, who, with his wife and child, occupied a room in the north wing, was awakened by the frenzied barking of his watch dog. On investigating, Jones found the corridor outside his room filled with smoke. He got his family out of the building and turned in the alarm.

Fire Chief Baldry, seeing how serious the fire was, asked for assistance from Niagara Falls, New York. The heroic efforts of firemen from both cities, however, were in vain. As the Niagara Falls *Review* reported: "A high swirling wind fanned the flames into one great blaze and the huge crowd watched the great structure turn into a giant torch, and saw the walls gradually buckle and fail, while the embers were carried long distances."

Eight lines of hose were in constant use for 48 hours, pouring some ten million litres (2,200,000 gallons) of water on the building.

The nearby Fox Head Inn supplied coffee and sandwiches to the police and firemen who were "drenched to the bone and smoked almost out of recognition."

The loss was estimated at a million dollars, while the cause was never determined.

And so, a second Clifton Hotel passed from the Niagara scene. It was the end of an era.

This story has an interesting sequel. The former hotel site as well as an adjoining parcel of land on the north side of the property was purchased by Harry Oakes, (later Sir Harry) a mining magnate who lived in Niagara Falls at the time.

In 1934, Oakes, who was a member of The Niagara Parks Commission, presented this valuable site to the Commission in exchange for a small piece of land above the steep hill behind Queen Victoria Park. Delighted at receiving this prime property, the Parks Commission decided to use the site to create a garden theatre that would be named in honour of Harry Oakes. Work began in 1935.

Oakes Garden Theatre was designed as an amphitheatre. It is fan-shaped with the circular stage so placed that the panorama of the Falls forms a natural backdrop. At the rear is a curved pergola connecting two open pavilions, one oriented on the axis of the Horseshoe Falls and the other on that of the American Falls.

A beautiful blend of architectural and horticultural skills, Oakes Garden Theatre was officially opened on September 18, 1937.

Oakes Garden Theatre at the foot of Clifton Hill as it looked shortly after the official opening in September 1937. This had previously been the site of the Clifton Hotels.

Sherman Zavitz Collection.

William Kondrat: An Incredible Swim

67

On the evening of July 17, 1933, Harold Brooker was on duty at the Spanish Aero Car, the famous cable car ride across the Niagara River Whirlpool. Suddenly, he noticed a man trying to get his attention from behind a bush some distance down the side of the Niagara Gorge. When he reached the spot, Brooker got the surprise of his life, for the man, naked and exhausted, told him that he just swam through the Lower (or Whirlpool) Rapids and Whirlpool of the Niagara River.

William Kondrat, who survived a swim through the treacherous Whirlpool in 1933.

Local History Department, Niagara Falls, New York, Public Library.

Astonished, Brooker managed to find a pair of overalls and then drove the very lucky young man to the Niagara Falls, Ontario, police headquarters. On the way the swimmer identified himself as William Kondrat, 18, of Chatham, New Jersey.

When questioned by the officers, Kondrat related his story. He and a friend, Arthur Hecht, had been hitchhiking to Chicago to see the Century of Progress Exposition being held there. They had arrived in Niagara Falls, New York, the previous Saturday, and finding themselves very low in funds, had obtained permission to sleep that night and the next at the police station.

On the following Monday, the two young men went to the northern part of the city to catch a westbound freight train. While in the area, they managed to get a handout from a small restaurant. They asked the owner where they might go to have a swim and were told of a pathway that went down the side of the gorge to the old *Maid of the Mist* landing, a short distance upstream from the Whirlpool Rapids Bridge.

The two friends easily found the spot. Kondrat, a powerful swimmer, stripped and entered the water, unaware that just a short distance downstream was one of the most violent stretches of white water in the world.

He swam about two-thirds of the way across the river. Then, as Kondrat later reported, "I suddenly thought of swimming across to Canada, as I had never been in that country and wanted to say that I had been there. When I had nearly reached the Canadian shore I discovered that I was in a swift current and decided to turn back." This he quickly found was impossible to do, and shortly after William Kondrat was shot into the Whirlpool Rapids.

Realizing he couldn't reach either bank, he put all his energy into keeping his head above water. "I simply went along, keeping my strength instead of struggling." A steady nerve, his outstanding ability as a swimmer and incredible luck saw him through.

Then came the Whirlpool. As Kondrat described it, "Three times I was carried into the vortex and pulled 40 or 50 feet beneath the surface. As I tried to fight my way to the top, I could see immense bubbles and the sun, filtered through the green water, being transformed into all the colours of the spectrum. Somewhere I had read that the way to escape an undertow was to swim with it. I tried that and suddenly was tossed 30 feet into the air." After several desperate attempts to reach land, he finally caught hold of a rock and pulled himself out. Kondrat later described his condition at this point: "My arms were virtually useless. My lungs were full of water. I had the worst headache I've ever experienced. My brain was in a fog and I fell over, but didn't faint. And the strange part of it was, when help reached me, the first thing I wanted was a drink of water."

Witnesses to the swim later verified his story. William Kondrat had accidentally achieved what no other swimmer had ever done. Wearing no safety gear whatsoever, he had gone through the Lower Rapids and Whirlpool of the Niagara River and lived to tell about it.

Later that night Kondrat was taken across the Whirlpool Rapids Bridge and turned over to Niagara Falls, New York, authorities. They arrested and jailed him on charges of vagrancy and unlawfully swimming in the river. He was released the next morning, the judge commenting that Kondrat was "too courageous a man to be treated as a tramp."

For a time, he became a local celebrity. The Lafayette Theatre in Buffalo, for example, hired him to tell his story to their audiences under the billing "The Tarzan of the Waters."

William Kondrat added an exciting and unbelievable chapter to the Niagara story. It had been a remarkable exploit that has never been duplicated.

"A Weary Groan": Death of a Bridge

68

One of the most dramatic events in the history of Niagara Falls took place on January 27, 1938.

During the preceding few days, a massive ice bridge, the biggest anyone had ever seen, developed in the Niagara River immediately below the Falls. The gorge was soon choked with 18 metres (60 feet) or more of ice, raising the water level more than 10.5 metres (35 feet) above normal.

It was a destructive and unstoppable force. Ice and water smashed their way through the windows of the Ontario Power Plant, located alongside the river near the base of the Horseshoe Falls. In a short time the building was inundated, making it necessary to shut down all 15 of the plant's generators.

A little further downstream, the two *Maid of the Mist* boats were pushed off their winter berths on the Canadian shore. At the same time, their docking area was destroyed and the caretaker's home knocked off its foundation. While all this was happening, serious concern was developing over the fate of the 40-year-old Falls View Bridge. This span, originally

Niagara's famous Falls View (or Upper Arch) Bridge fell onto the Niagara River ice on January 27, 1938. These photos show the bridge just before, during, and just after the collapse.
Sherman Zavitz Collection.

known as the Steel Arch Bridge, was located just slightly upstream from the present Rainbow Bridge. Ice was quickly piling up against its abutments and hinge supports, exerting tremendous pressure that was gradually weakening the structure.

Bridge maintenance crews had been called out at 4 a.m., January 26, to try and clear away the ice from around the abutments. It was a futile effort, however, especially since more and more ice kept pouring over the Falls. As soon as there was enough light, engineers examined the span and discovered that some of the girders were already beginning to buckle. Not long after, the bridge began to sag slightly at the American end.

Clearly, the Falls View Bridge was doomed. At 9:15 that morning, it was closed and the deathwatch began. News of its imminent demise spread quickly, attracting large crowds, including many newspaper reporters, to the scene.

The end came at about 4:14 p.m. (eyewitnesses gave slightly varying times) the next day, Thursday, January 27, 1938. The Niagara Falls, Ontario, *Review*, in its edition for the following day, described it this way: "With startling suddenness, and what sounded like a weary groan, the mighty structure sagged and fell into the gorge. There was not a great deal of noise as the 2,600 tons of steel and 300 tons of wood, which comprised the framework and floor of the bridge, sank to rest, and onlookers scarcely believed their eyes as they saw the destruction of the once proud span which now lies in the shape of a great twisted "W" on the ice bridge."

The paper also struck a nostalgic note: "In the minds of countless thousands of persons in every nook and corner of the continent are memories of the Falls View Bridge. Honeymooners of the horse and buggy days and the present era of high-speed autos and streamlined trains have viewed the Cataracts from the deck of the famous structure." (It was, in fact, often called the Honeymoon Bridge.)

The following Sunday, Niagara Falls experienced one of the busiest days in its history up to that time, as thousands came by car, train, electric railway, bus or on foot to see the remains of the Falls View Bridge lying shattered on the ice. As the *Review* reported in its Monday edition, "All day both sides of the river were black with people."

Experts warned that if the wreckage was allowed to drop into the river in one piece following the breakup of the ice, it could become an underwater barrier. This would impede the flow of the ice.

To avoid this potential problem, a plan was created to divide the bridge into a number of sections. Over the next few days, a team of workmen cut some of the span's girders.

Then, after this first stage of the operation was completed, a total of 300 kilograms (660 pounds) of dynamite was placed at strategic spots along the length of the wreckage. This was detonated at 2:30 a.m. on February 5, resulting in a blast so powerful it broke about $10,000 worth of windows in the area.

The bridge was now cut into six sections, although to the casual observer there was little change in its appearance.

During the following few weeks, a portion of the steel and wood from the approach section lying on the Canadian side of the gorge bank was salvaged. Many souvenir hunters also visited the site.

The wreckage remained on view until April 12, when the ice bridge began to break up. The approach section that had been resting partly on both the American bank and the ice, slipped into the water shortly after seven o'clock that morning.

Over the next several hours, all the other pieces but one sank into the river close to where they had been lying.

The final section, which was near the Canadian shore, remained until the afternoon when it was carried downriver on a massive piece of ice. About 4:05, amid loud cracking noises as the ice underneath broke up, it disappeared under the water over 1.6 kilometres (1 mile) below the Falls.

The Falls View Bridge had passed into history. It was replaced by the Rainbow Bridge, which opened on November 1, 1941.

Jimmy Stewart: A Legendary Movie Star Visits Niagara Falls

69

The General Brock Hotel (now called the Crowne Plaza) has hosted many celebrities since its opening in 1929. Among them was the legendary movie star, Jimmy Stewart, who visited Niagara Falls in 1940.

Sherman Zavitz Collection.

The 1997 death of Jimmy Stewart removed another link with Hollywood's golden era. The film legend, whose first screen appearance came in 1935, was one of the most successful and respected actors in the history of the motion picture industry. A veteran of over 75 movies, he was particularly well-known for playing the somewhat bashful, stubbornly honest, ordinary citizen in such classics as *Mr. Smith Goes to Washington*.

Jimmy Stewart, along with his parents and two sisters, paid a visit to Niagara Falls on September 6 and 7, 1940. They came here following a two-week fishing trip in the Lake Temagami area of northern Ontario. Just before his holiday, Stewart had finished making *The Philadelphia Story*, a movie for which he would receive an Academy Award for best actor.

Word of his impending arrival at the General Brock Hotel (since renamed the Crowne Plaza) had spread all over Niagara Falls during the morning of September 6, so when Stewart made his appearance at the hotel that afternoon he was met by a large crowd of autograph seekers.

Later, the actor and his family viewed the Falls and toured along the Niagara River before having dinner as the guests of the Brock's manager, Ronald Peck, and his wife.

The following morning as the Stewarts stepped from a General Brock elevator, they were greeted by a reporter from the Niagara Falls, Ontario, *Review* who, to his astonishment, "received a warm and cordial welcome from the family," as he later wrote.

The reporter had quite a talk with the renowned actor, who is described as 6 feet tall (1.8 metres), wearing a pinstriped grey suit along with brown sport shoes, and looking in person "exactly as he does on the screen."

Stewart was delighted with the Falls, commenting that they were "the most picturesque sight" he had ever seen, and that he was "thrilled to death" with the scenery along the Niagara River. He also mentioned that he had enjoyed his vacation in northern Ontario and was particularly impressed with the beauty of that area.

When asked about his own favorite actors and actresses, Stewart felt that Spencer Tracy and Margaret Sullivan were, in his opinion, "superior to any in Hollywood."

Autograph seekers literally mobbed him that morning as well, but Stewart took it all in stride, noting that he never got tired of signing his name and was amazed at how many people recognized him.

Much of Stewart's popularity over the years had to do with his easy charm and down-to-earth manner. The *Review* reporter was obviously aware of this when he wrote: "Mr. Stewart is a modest chap. He refuses to discuss his success in pictures and does not make out to be different than any ordinary person. An interesting point about him is his desire to stand and chat with his admirers."

Later that day, the Stewart family left Niagara Falls for the United States. It seems safe to say that a number of good memories of their Ontario experience went with them.

Winston Churchill:
A Wartime Stop at Niagara

70

Winston Churchill (later knighted), with his daughter Mary, photographed while on a brief stop at Niagara Falls in 1943. Standing beside Mary is Maxim T. Gray, General Manager of The Niagara Parks Commission.

The Niagara Parks Commission.

Sir Winston Churchill was unquestionably one of the twentieth century's major figures.

During his long lifetime Churchill visited Niagara Falls on three occasions. The first was in December, 1900, while on a lecture tour of North America. He came again on August 18, 1929, while on a vacation showing his son, Randolph, some of the wonders on this side of the Atlantic.

Churchill's last visit here was during World War II. He had come to Canada, accompanied by his wife and daughter, Mary, to attend a War Conference at Quebec City with President Roosevelt, and to also meet with the Canadian Prime Minister Mackenzie King. The British leader decided to take a day away from meetings and show Mary the splendour of Niagara Falls.

Wartime secrecy prevented any publicity of the visit, except to officials. As a result, only a guard of Royal Canadian Mounted Police, Mayor George Inglis, his wife, and a scattering of other people were on hand to greet the famous guests as they arrived by special train at the Queen Victoria Park Station at the top of Clifton Hill at 8:45 on the morning of August 12, 1943. Churchill appeared from the train complete with his cigar, cane, and flashing his famous "V for Victory" sign.

They were then driven through Queen Victoria Park to Table Rock where Maxim T. Gray, General Manager of The Niagara Parks Commission, greeted them. After viewing the Falls, which Mary pronounced "absolutely thrilling," the motorcade proceeded along River Road and the Parkway to the Spanish (now Whirlpool) Aero Car for a look at the Whirlpool, and then on to Queenston Heights, site of the battle of the same name during the War of 1812.

Here Churchill and his daughter viewed the lower Niagara River from the Queenston Heights Restaurant. When asked if he would like to climb nearby, lofty, Brock's Monument, Churchill replied, "It wouldn't be good for me at all." He then asked why no monument equal to Brock's had been erected to Sir Roger Hale Sheaffe who had actually won the battle on the Heights, following Brock's death, on October 13, 1812. Answering his own question, he suggested it was because he wasn't killed.

Churchill and his daughter were then returned to their train and headed back to Quebec City.

Undoubtedly, the ninety-minute visit to Niagara was a pleasant interlude during the serious days of 1943.

Winston Churchill declined the invitation to climb Brock's Monument, but he and his daughter enjoyed the view of the lower Niagara River from the Queenston Heights Restaurant, seen at the right.
John Burtniak Collection.

71

Shirley Temple:
The Relighting of Niagara Falls

Throughout the 1930s and 40s, Shirley Temple was one of Hollywood's most famous celebrities. In fact, each year from 1935 to 1938, she was voted the number one movie star in the United States.

Shirley began her film career in 1931, at the age of three. She went on to charm and entertain theatre audiences during the Depression years, becoming one of the most popular and famous of all child stars. Her blond ringlets, singing, dancing and appealing manner captivated millions, and helped to raise people's spirits during a difficult period.

Shirley continued to make movies as a teenager during the 1940s. In October 1944, while World War II was still raging, she made a brief visit to Canada, where several appearances had been scheduled for her to help promote the sale of war bonds.

Wearing her mink coat, Shirley Temple poses on the balcony of the Victoria Park Restaurant (now called Victoria Park Place) on the evening of October 22, 1944.
Courtesy of the Niagara Parks Archives.

Her first stop was Ottawa, the nation's capital, where she took part in launching Canada's seventh Victory Loan Drive. During the visit she had a private conversation with one of her greatest admirers, Prime Minister W.L. Mackenzie King.

Shirley, along with her parents and publicity agent, then travelled by train to Niagara Falls, Ontario, arriving on the morning of Sunday, October 22.

That afternoon, escorted by Niagara Falls Mayor George Inglis and other officials, the 16 year-old star was shown the sights along the Niagara River, including the Spanish (now Whirlpool) Aero Car, which she felt was "quite impressive." She also visited Oak Hall, which at that time was being used as a

RCAF Convalescent Home. (Formerly the residence of Sir Harry Oakes, Oak Hall is now the administration headquarters of The Niagara Parks Commission.)

The tour was followed by a tea at the residence of Fred Cairns, and his wife, Tillie. Cairns was the manager of the local Borden's Dairy. The Cairns' elegant, two-storey brick house where Shirley was a guest on that October afternoon in 1944, still stands on the southeast corner of Simcoe Street and Second Avenue. The Hollywood star apparently felt quite at home there, even answering the kitchen doorbell when the hostess didn't hear it ring.

Speaking to a reporter during the tea, she confided that even though it would likely be awhile before she married, "It is a toss-up between here and Hawaii for my honeymoon."

Following dinner at the General Brock Hotel (now the Crowne Plaza), Shirley was driven into Queen Victoria Park where a huge crowd had gathered to see her. The reporter noted that she was wearing "a smart black jersey dress with jet black buttons under a mink coat, and a black hat over her golden hair."

After reaching the Victoria Park Restaurant, Shirley presided at a ceremony to celebrate the resumption of the Falls being illuminated. This was part of a program to open the local Victory Loan Drive.

Although there had been several early attempts at lighting the Falls, it was not until 1925 that permanent illumination began. This nightly spectacle became extremely popular.

During most of World War II, however, the lights were turned off in order to conserve electricity for war production purposes. By October 1944, with victory felt to be near, it was decided that the Falls could once again be regularly illuminated, and Shirley Temple helped to mark this significant occasion.

While in Queen Victoria Park that night, Shirley had a conversation with two Air Force men who had asked her for an autograph. They happened to mention that they were about to hitchhike to Hamilton, Ontario, about 65 kilometres (40 miles) to the west. Following the lighting ceremony, Shirley was going to be driven to the same city in order to catch a train to Chicago. She offered the two surprised airmen a ride. Naturally, they couldn't turn down an invitation like that, and so had the pleasure of travelling to Hamilton with Shirley Temple.

Navy Island: Niagara's Choice for the UN Headquarters

72

An artist's representation of what the United Nations headquarters on Navy Island might look like, as featured in a 1945 promotional booklet. The view is looking north, with mist rising from both the Canadian Falls (just left of centre) and the American Falls. The Canadian mainland is at the far left, while Grand Island, New York is in the foreground.

Niagara Falls, Ontario, Public Library.

During the spring of 1945, an historic conference took place in San Francisco. Delegates from 50 nations met there and over several months worked out a charter for a new organization then taking shape on the world scene that was to be known as the United Nations.

Born at the close of the Second World War, the UN was created, as the charter states, "to make a peace which will banish the scourge and terror of war."

Since then, it has not only played a vital role in promoting peace and cooperation among the countries of the world, but has also been a centre for identifying the common problems of humankind.

One difficulty that faced the founding members of the United Nations was just where the headquarters should be established. Naturally, there were many contenders for the honour. Paris, London, Geneva, Chicago and San Francisco, among others, extended invitations.

Not to be left out, however, was the Niagara Falls area. An international committee was formed, made up of individuals from Western New York and Ontario's Niagara Peninsula, to promote Navy Island as the UN headquarters. At a large dinner meeting held at the Victoria Park Restaurant in Niagara Falls on August 8, 1945, Louis Blake Duff of Welland, Ontario, and Harry Hooker, president of the Hooker Electro-Chemical Company of Niagara Falls, New York, were elected co-chairmen of the committee.

Navy Island, 126 hectares (315 acres) in size, sits in the Niagara River about 4.8 kilometres (3 miles) above the Horseshoe Falls. It belongs to Canada.

The committee felt that it was the ideal site for this new world body then being formed. The island was located in an area of exceptional beauty and fame as well as along the border to two great and peaceful nations. The area also had excellent accessibility and a pleasant climate. If selected, arrangements would be made to deed the island to the United Nations, following which two bridges would be constructed to reach it, one from nearby Grand Island and the other from the Canadian mainland near Chippawa.

All these facts were clearly laid out in meetings with various levels of government on both sides of the border, and to members of the UN Advisory Committee which was in charge of recommending a location. New York Governor Thomas Dewey and President Harry Truman endorsed the idea. Canadian Prime Minister Mackenzie King, however, did not.

As part of the promotion, the local committee, at its own expense, produced a large and beautiful booklet. Some 3,000 copies were printed and sent to UN delegates and other influential individuals and agencies around the world.

The centre of the booklet featured an artist's depiction, a double-page spread, of what Navy Island could look like with the UN buildings on it. The connecting bridges are also shown, while in the distance is the mist rising from the Falls.

Despite the committee's energetic efforts, Navy Island lost out. The choice fell to New York City when the Rockefeller brothers offered 10.4 hectares (26 acres) on Manhattan's east side. The site had formerly been a slum and slaughterhouse property.

Navy Island has remained a wilderness area. If the United Nations had decided to locate there, however, it is interesting to not only visualize what the island's appearance would be today, but to speculate on what the UN's presence in this area would have meant to the city of Niagara Falls.

A Television First at Niagara Falls

73

A bit of television history was made in 1948. On Sunday, September 12 that year, WBEN-TV (now WIVB) of Buffalo made a live telecast from Niagara Falls, Ontario, showing the American and Canadian Falls, Oakes Garden Theatre, Queen Victoria Park, the Rainbow Bridge and the *Maid of the Mist*. This was the first time the famous cataracts had been shown on television. It was also the first international telecast ever made in the Americas.

The hour-long program was a considerable technological achievement for the time. Cameras were mounted on an eleventh-floor balcony of the General Brock (now Crowne Plaza) Hotel. This meant that 45 metres (150 feet) of cable had to be brought up from the ground level. A parabolic antenna, for transmitting the picture signal by microwave relay, was installed on the hotel's roof. The receiving

Mr. and Mrs. Cothrell Thompson of Elkton, Maryland, were married on September 11, 1948. The following day they became the first Niagara Falls honeymooners to be interviewed on television during the first telecast ever made at Niagara. This picture, taken the next day, shows the couple at the Spanish Aero Car.

The Niagara Falls, Ontario, *Review*, September 12, 1948.

antenna was located on top of the Statler Hotel in downtown Buffalo where WBEN had its studios. Sound was sent over special telephone wires.

In 1948 television was still in its infancy. WBEN was the only station in Buffalo and, in fact, had been on the air for just a few months. (Canada wouldn't have a station for another four years.) Since few people in the Niagara area owned a television set, this remarkable program had a relatively small audience.

For those who did view it, however, they saw what the *Buffalo Evening News* described as "the most sensational telecast ever attempted."

Officials from both sides of the border were invited by the Greater Niagara Chamber of Commerce to see the show on screens arranged by RCA Victor of Toronto in the Blue Room of the General Brock Hotel.

During the program, messages were read from Ontario Premier George Drew and New York State Governor Thomas Dewey. WBEN announcer, Ed Dinsmore, talked with Maxim T. Gray, General Manager of The Niagara Parks Commission, and Francis Seyfried of the Niagara Frontier State Park Commission.

The Rainbow Carillon was also featured as part of the production, and there was an interview with a honeymooning couple, Mr. and Mrs. Cothrell Thompson of Elkton, Maryland. They had been married only the day before and became the first Niagara Falls honeymooners to be on television.

Today, such a program would be considered commonplace, but in 1948 it was a very unique and exciting experience for participants and viewers alike.

William "Red" Hill, Jr.: Courage on the Niagara

74

One of the most dramatic and dangerous acts of courage on the Niagara River took place on Friday, May 24, 1946. Three days before, Walter Sinclair, of Niagara Falls, New York, had plunged over the American Cataract. Since then his lifeless body had lain wedged in the rocks near the base of the Falls, about 23

Members of the Hill family were well-known Niagara rivermen. Here, William "Red" Hill, Sr. (at left) wears some of his lifesaving medals as he shakes the hand of his son, William "Red" Jr. The photo likely dates to 1931. Both father and son became famous for daring rescues and for their stunts on the Niagara River.

Sherman Zavitz Collection.

metres (75 feet) north of the closest Cave of the Winds platform, and approximately 15 metres (50 feet) from the river's edge.

While in plain view of thousands of visitors, removal of the body seemed to be impossible due to the great danger involved. Neither the U.S. Coast Guard nor the Niagara Falls, New York, Fire Department had the equipment for such a recovery operation. *Maid of the Mist* Company officials said that the dangerous currents and rocks would make it impossible to reach the body with one of their little steamers. As well, police prohibited any attempt to crawl across the rocks from the Cave of the Winds stairway.

It seemed as though the body would have to remain where it was.

At this point, however, William "Red" Hill Junior stepped forward and volunteered to make the hazardous recovery. Members of the Hill family, from Niagara Falls, Ontario, had long been famous for their intimate knowledge of the Niagara River and for having made many rescues. On this particular occasion Red was joined by his brother, Norman "Corky" and another noted riverman, Roy Healey.

In the late afternoon, the three men set out across the river in a rowboat headed for a large rock at the foot of the American Falls. It was not to be an easy task. As the Niagara Falls, Ontario, *Review* reported: "Time and time again the boat was nearly swamped by the churning, racing waters and the boiling current. For more than half an hour the trio struggled to make a landing on the slippery, spray-drenched rock toward which they were aiming."

The men finally reached their goal, climbed onto the rock and hauled up their boat. They then moved further along the foot of the Falls to another large rock which they used as their base of operations.

Healey, who wore an artificial leg, stayed on this rock to handle the ropes which the two Hill brothers held as they began to struggle on through the raging, waist-deep water. They had moved away from Healey only a short distance when he suddenly began to slip off the rock. Only the swift action of Red Hill, who grabbed the falling man by the shoulder of his coat, saved him.

After reorganizing, the operation continued as the brothers picked their way precariously through the rushing water and over slippery rocks, while almost blinded by spray and deafened by the roar of the Falls. Above them great crowds tensely watched the unfolding drama.

After more than an hour, Red Hill succeeded in reaching the body and pried it loose from the rocks. It was then lowered to Healey who fastened the body to the large rock on which he had been stationed. The Hill brothers carefully worked their way down to Healey and then over to the rock where their boat had been left.

Launching their craft and securing the body to it was very difficult. At one point the body slipped and would have been lost but for lightning moves by the three rivermen.

Finally, they were able to set out and rowed through the vicious current to the American *Maid of the Mist* landing. The recovery was completed successfully and all three men were rightly given great praise.

Five years later, Red Hill, who had already twice successfully navigated the Niagara River's Whirlpool Rapids in a barrel, decided to go over the Horseshoe Falls. For this stunt he put together a contraption named "The Thing." It was constructed of 13 large heavy-duty inner tubes held together by straps of canvas

webbing. All of this was encased in fish net. Hill was held inside by a harness. The trip took place on August 5, 1951, and attracted thousands of spectators.

"The Thing," however, was no match for the power of Niagara and was already disintegrating before it slipped over the edge of the cataract. It was a tragic finale for William "Red" Hill Junior. This time it was his body that had to be recovered.

A group of Red Hill Jr.'s close friends (from left to right): Fred E. Smith, Danny White and Ron Smart, burning the remains of the inner tube barrel.

John Burtniak Collection.

Sherman Zavitz Collection.

During June 1952, Hollywood came to Niagara Falls, Ontario.

It was an exciting time for the city as it became the setting for the Twentieth Century-Fox movie *Niagara*.

Not only was extensive filming done around the Falls, but scenes were also shot at city hall, the old post office at the corner of Park Street and Zimmerman Avenue, the bus depot (which at that time was located at the Rainbow Bridge), the hospital (then on Jepson Street), and in Chippawa. The Rainbow Bridge Carillon also figured prominently in the movie.

Marilyn Monroe poses in Queen Victoria Park with the American Falls in the background. She was in Niagara Falls during June 1952 for the making of *Niagara*.

Sherman Zavitz Collection.

Some residents had the thrill of being hired as extras or bit players.

A motel, or more exactly the facade of a motel, was constructed in Queen Victoria Park, opposite the American Falls. Named the Rainbow Motel, the six-unit building was constructed by local contractor Arthur Jolley. A number of the movie's pivotal scenes took place at this 'motel.'

For about three weeks, Niagara Falls had an extra attraction that for many residents and visitors rivaled the Falls for attention.

As the Niagara Falls, Ontario *Review* noted in its June 5, 1952, edition, "Thousands of people visited Queen Victoria Park yesterday and today, but nary a glance did they cast toward the mighty cataracts. All attention was focused on the 'Rainbow Motel' where Twentieth Century-Fox was shooting scenes for the full-length technicolour film *Niagara*."

The movie, a suspense drama, stared Marilyn Monroe, Joseph Cotten and Jean Peters. Also featured were Casey Adams, Lurene Tuttle and Don Wilson, who was Jack Benny's announcer for many years. Along with the cast, some 50 crewmembers were present as part of the $2,000,000 production. The director was Henry Hathaway.

While all the stars of the film received considerable attention from the public during their time here, the main focus was on Marilyn. The Niagara Falls *Review* wrote, "Milling crowds are often around her."

Although she had previously appeared in many movies, her first lead role came in *Niagara*. The film was a turning point in her career and was to win her international stardom. Ten years and two months after leaving Niagara Falls, Marilyn Monroe died at the age of 36. Official records state she took her own life. Some, however, still question this verdict.

During breaks in the filming, Marilyn was able to do a bit of sightseeing, which included a stroll through Queen Victoria Park, shopping at the Table Rock store and an impromptu ride on the *Maid of the Mist*. She was also a guest of the Oneida Company for a tour of their silverware plant which was on Falls Avenue where Casino Niagara is now located.

Local headquarters for Twentieth Century-Fox was the General Brock Hotel (now called the Crowne Plaza). This is also where the cast members stayed. Marilyn was in room 801.

Most of the filming here was finished by June 20, with interior shooting scheduled for the following three weeks in Hollywood. Before leaving, Henry Hathaway expressed his thanks to the residents and business people of Niagara Falls for their hospitality and cooperation.

Marilyn by the rocks near the Canadian Maid of the Mist landing. The Horseshoe Falls can be seen in the background.

Niagara Falls, Ontario, Public Library.

As the Niagara Falls, Ontario, *Review* reported, he went on to say, "Everyone has been extremely kind and cordial to all of us. We have enjoyed our brief stay here and return home with memories of a gracious community and beautiful country."

The Rainbow Motel was put up for sale to the highest bidder. Arthur Jolley's offer was the best submitted, so he was able to purchase and then dismantle the building he had originally constructed. For years after, many tourists arriving here tried to register at the motel where Marilyn Monroe and Joseph Cotten (who played her husband) had stayed.

Niagara had its Canadian premiere in Niagara Falls on Wednesday, January 28, 1953, at the Seneca Theatre on Queen Street. None of the movie's stars could be present, but Twentieth Century-Fox did send along a popular actor of the time, Dale Robertson, to add some extra excitement to the festivities. The film went on to be a great success at the box office, earning five times its cost.

Niagara, is the story of a scheming wife (Monroe), who brings her husband, a war-shocked veteran, to Niagara Falls and plots with her lover to have him pushed into the Falls.

Jean Peters and Casey Adams play the happy honeymooners who become involved with Cotten's character and thwart his wife's plans.

Publicity at the time enthused, "Marilyn Monroe and Niagara, a raging torrent of emotion that even nature can't control."

The *Review* in writing about the film noted, "It provides an abundant display of Marilyn Monroe's physical allurements and at the same time has the scenic splendor of Niagara Falls as a background for the emotional turbulence she herself provokes."

Roger Woodward:
A Day for a Miracle

76

Saturday, July 9, 1960, became a day for a double miracle at Niagara Falls. As Tony Fredo of the Niagara Falls, Ontario, *Review* wrote, "Death missed its cue twice."

It was around 10:30 that morning when seven-year-old Roger Woodward and his sister Deanne, 17, set out with a family friend, James Honeycutt, for a boat ride on the upper Niagara River. The trio, all from Niagara Falls, New York, began their journey about eight kilometres (five miles) above the Falls.

On July 9, 1960, seven-year-old Roger Woodward became the only person in recorded history to accidentally go over Niagara Falls and survive. This photo, taken by a passenger on the *Maid of the Mist*, shows Roger in the water (insided added circle) shortly after his plunge over the Horseshoe Falls, seen in the background.

Tony Fredo Photo: *Niagara Parks Archives.*

Honeycutt, 40, headed his 4.2-metre (14-foot) aluminum boat, which contained two life jackets, downriver. Apparently, he was not concerned when they passed the International Control Works - the point of no return. In fact, Honeycutt did not seem to realize the danger he and his passengers were in until they were about 790 metres (a half-mile) from the brink of the Horseshoe Falls.

They could see a group of tourists standing at Terrapin Point on Goat Island. Now frantic, Honeycutt turned the boat and tried to head through the rapids for Goat Island. Suddenly, the small motor began to race wildly and then stall after losing or stripping a pin.

Telling Deanna to put on her life jacket (Roger was already wearing his), Honeycutt then tried to row through the violent water. Terrified, Roger screamed. "We're going to die!"

The rapids struck the boat, tossing it into the air and throwing its passengers into the torrent. Honeycutt was able to grasp Roger for only a moment before the force of the water tore them apart. Seconds later the two were swept over the Falls.

When the boat capsized, Deanne was at first able to hang onto the overturned craft. However the rapids quickly wrenched her away from it and propelled her towards the brink of the Falls, close to Terrapin Point.

John Hayes, a policeman from Union Township, New Jersey, who was standing at the point, reacted instantly. He climbed through the guardrail and seized the screaming girl's hand, while hooking his leg over the rail to keep from being pulled in. Desperately holding onto the girl with his right hand, Hayes yelled for help.

John Quattrochi, also from New Jersey, responded to the call. He jumped over the rail and grabbed Deanne's other hand. Together, the two men pulled her out of the water and over the rail – about 4.5 metres (15 feet) from the brink.

At the same time, just below the Falls, another drama was being played out.

Having reached to within 60 metres (200 feet) of the centre section of the Horseshoe Falls, Captain Clifford Keech of the *Maid of the Mist* was about to turn the little boat when he spied something in the water. Keech later related for the *Review* what happened next: "I couldn't believe my eyes. I saw the boy come popping out of the water, probably just after going over the Falls. His orange life jacket attracted my attention first. When the boy saw us, he started calling for help. We had to circle around several times because the current kept taking him further from the boat. It took us about three

Rescued! Astride a *Maid of the Mist* life ring, Roger is about to be pulled aboard the famous excursion boat by Jack Hopkins, a deckhand.

Maid of the Mist Steamboat Company.

minutes to bring him in. My first mate, Murray Hartling, and a deckhand, Jack Hopkins, tossed him a life preserver. They helped him aboard. He kept crying about his sister. We looked around for a while but couldn't see anyone. I've been making this trip for 38 years. I've never seen anything like it."

After the *Maid of the Mist* docked, Roger was rushed to Greater Niagara General Hospital by ambulance. An examination showed, however, that except for some bruises and soreness, he was fine.

At Memorial Hospital in Niagara Falls, New York, Deanna was also found to be uninjured, although she was suffering from shock, likely because she was more aware of the immense danger that she and her brother had been in.

Roger said all he could remember was "falling a long way."

A few hours later, both children were well enough to pose for pictures and talk to reporters. James Honeycutt was not as lucky. His body was recovered four days later.

While speaking about Roger's miracle of survival, Arthur Williams of the Niagara Frontier State Parks Commission noted, "It was a 100 million to one shot. It never happened before and it will never happen again."

Princess Diana:
The People's Princess Comes to Niagara

77

It was August 31, 1997. The tragic news from Paris that late summer Sunday caused millions the world over to gasp in disbelief. Diana, Princess of Wales, had been killed in a car crash.

Diana's natural charm, flair, compassion, beauty and wit, all complimented by a winning smile, had made her one of the most dazzling personalities of the time as well as among the most written about and photographed women of the 20th century.

Born Lady Diana Spencer on July 1, 1961, she married Prince Charles, heir to the British throne, on July 29, 1981. Held at St. Paul's Cathedral, London, the fairy tale wedding was televised to a worldwide audience of 750 million. Their first child, Prince William, was born in June 1982, and Prince Harry arrived two years later.

The late Princess Diana and her sons (left to right: Prince Henry (Harry) and Prince William) enjoyed the sights and sounds of Niagara Falls while on board the *Maid of the Mist* during their visit in October 1991.

George Bailey Collection.

The royal couple first visited Canada in 1983 and received a warm and enthusiastic welcome. Wherever they appeared there were plenty of cheers and signs that read, "We love you Chuck and Di."

It was during another Canadian visit in 1991 that Diana, along with her two sons, came to Niagara Falls. They arrived by helicopter from Toronto, where Charles had remained on business, at 11:30 a.m. on Saturday, October 26. They were first driven to Table Rock to view the Falls. A heavy mist was blowing over the area as the royal threesome, accompanied by various officials, briskly and eagerly walked to the railing, Diana taking Harry's hand while William went ahead.

Obviously excited, the boys ran back and forth between two of the binocular viewers to get an even closer look at the Falls. The wet conditions didn't bother them a bit, William commenting, "I think it's lovely. I don't mind the mist at all."

Suddenly the mist let up a bit, allowing a little sun to break through. At this point, Diana walked over to the thousand or so spectators. To the crowd's delight, not only did she begin to shake hands and talk to some of them, but William and Harry followed right along behind her doing the same thing.

After the walkabout and a trip through the Scenic Tunnels (now called Journey Behind the Falls), the three famous visitors were driven to the *Maid of the Mist* dock where they donned their blue waterproof coats and were then escorted to the upper deck of the *Maid of the Mist IV*. As the little boat headed out into the river, the princes waved to the crowds gathered along the upper banks of the gorge. William and Harry particularly enjoyed the *Maid of the Mist* trip since they were each given an opportunity to take the wheel and blow the whistle during the 20-minute ride.

Lunch was held in the Commissioners' Quarters of the Victoria Park Restaurant on the Canadian side. Diana, a vegetarian, ate a vegetable salad and some pasta, while her sons had cucumber, tomato and smoked salmon sandwiches. For dessert, each enjoyed a chocolate sundae.

The three-hour Niagara visit then over, Diana and the princes returned to Toronto by helicopter.

For most of those fortunate enough to have seen Diana that day, it was a never-to-be-forgotten experience. For them and millions of others, the "people's princess" will always have a special place in their hearts.

Princess Diana, Prince William and Prince Harry enjoy some refreshments on board the *Maid of the Mist*. George Bailey Collection.

Hugh Pattinson:
Niagara Falls' First Photographer

78

Using a daguerreotype camera, Hugh Pattinson of England took this picture and the one on the following page in the spring of 1840. They were the first photos every taken of Niagara Falls. This is a view of the American Falls.

Robinson Library, University of Newcastle, Newcastle upon Tyne, England.

A remarkable discovery took place in October 1997, when library staff at the University of Newcastle in Newcastle upon Tyne, England, opened an old box that had been sitting in one of the library's storerooms for around 70 years.

Inside the dust-covered carton, they found the very first pictures ever taken of Niagara Falls.

The eight images are daguerreotypes and are known to have been taken by Hugh Pattinson of England, who visited Niagara Falls in 1840. They had been given to the university by some of Pattinson's descendants during the 1920s, but were thought to have been accidentally destroyed some years ago.

Experts in photographic history know of Pattinson's pioneering work with daguerreotypes and say that his photos are not only the first of Niagara Falls, but the first taken in Canada, having been made only months after this early form of photography was available to the public.

The daguerreotype was the first practical method of photography and was named after its inventor, Louis Daguerre of France. He announced his discovery

Taken in 1840 from a balcony of the Clifton House Hotel, this was the first photograph of the Horseshoe (Canadian) Falls.

Robinson Library, University of Newcastle, Newcastle upon Tyne, England.

in 1839. To create a daguerreotype, the image was recorded on a copper plate coated with silver iodide, using an exposure time of 15 to 20 minutes.

Hugh Pattinson did not come to North America, however, just to take pictures. Born in 1796, he lived in the area around Newcastle upon Tyne for most of his life. He became a respected authority on many branches of science but was particularly skilled as a metallurgical chemist.

It was his knowledge in that area that actually brought him to this side of the Atlantic in late 1839. Pattinson had been asked to invest in what was publicized as a potentially valuable silver mine located in South Carolina, but wanted to inspect the site before committing himself. It is fortunate that he did since the mine turned out to be worthless.

After leaving South Carolina, he went to New York for a time and then to Upper Canada (Ontario) where he apparently visited relatives and did some touring before arriving at Niagara Falls in the spring of 1840.

Pattinson had brought a daguerreotype camera with him and set it up on a balcony of the Clifton House Hotel which stood where Oakes Garden Theatre is now located.

Pointing the camera directly at the Falls, he then proceeded to take the first photographic images of the world's most famous waterfall.

Back in England, Pattinson gave a lecture on the daguerreotype and showed his views of Niagara Falls at a meeting of the Literary Society of Newcastle upon Tyne on December 1, 1840.

The local newspaper reported that his pictures "were examined with considerable interest."

When one thinks about the incredible number of pictures of Niagara Falls that have been taken over the years, it is amazing to realize that the original ones still exist.

Selected Bibliography

Baltensperger, Peter. *Saints and Sinners of Niagara.* (Maple, ON: Belsten Publishing, 1982).

Berton, Pierre. *Niagara: A History of the Falls.* (Toronto: McClelland and Stewart, 1992).

Bird, Isabella Lucy. *The Englishwomen in America.* (Toronto: University of Toronto Press, 1965. Originally published by John Murray, London, England, 1856).

Byfield, Shadrach. "A Common Soldier's Account." In *Recollections of the War of 1812: Three Eyewitnesses' Accounts.* Edited by John Gellner. (Toronto: Baxter Publishing, 1964).

Cheney, Margaret. *Tesla: Man Out of Time.* (New York: Barnes and Noble Books, 1981).

Coté, Richard N. *Theodosia Burr Alston: Portrait of a Prodigy.* (Mount Pleasant, S.C.: Corinthian Books, 2003).

Cruikshank, Ernest A. (ed.). *The Documentary History of the Campaign upon the Niagara Frontier, 1812-1814.* (Niagara Falls: The Lundy's Lane Historical Society, 1896-1908). 9 vols.

DeVeaux, Samuel. *The Falls of Niagara, or Tourist's Guide to the Wonders of Nature.* (Buffalo: William B. Hayden, 1839).

Dickens, Charles. *American Notes for General Circulation.* (London: Chapman and Hall, 1842).

Dictionary of Canadian Biography. (Toronto: University of Toronto Press 1966-90), various volumes.

Dow, Charles Mason. *Anthology and Bibliography of Niagara Falls.* (Albany: State of New York, 1921), 2 vols.

Duff, Louis Blake. *The County Kerchief.* (Toronto: Ryerson Press, 1949).

Duff, Louis Blake. "Samuel Chandler of St. Johns." Welland County Historical Society *Papers and Records.* (Welland, ON.), vol. 5 (1938). pp. 115-149.

Ellmann, Richard. *Oscar Wilde.* (London: Penguin Books, 1988).

Fryer, Mary Beacock. *Elizabeth Poshtuma Simcoe, 1762-1850; A Biography.* (Toronto: Dundurn Press, 1989).

Graham, M.H. *The Tiger of Canada West.* (Toronto: Clarke, Irwin, 1962).

Graves, Donald E. *Soldiers of 1814: American Enlisted Men's Memoirs of the Niagara Campaign.* (Youngstown, N.Y: Old Fort Niagara Association, 1995).

Graves, Donald E. (ed.) *Merry Hearts Make Light Days: The War of 1812 Journal of Lieutenant John Le Couteur; 104th Foot.* (Ottawa: Carleton University Press, 1993).

Green, Ernest. "John De Cou, Pioneer." Ontario Historical Society *Papers and Records.* (Toronto), vol. 22 (1925), pp. 92-116.

Greenhill, Ralph, and Mahoney, Thomas D. *Niagara.* (Toronto: University of Toronto Press, 1969).

Guillet, Edwin C. *The Lives and Times of the Patriots.* (Toronto: University of Toronto Press, 1968).

Hoy, Claire. *Canadians in the Civil War.* (Toronto: McArthur & Company, 2004).

Innis, Mary Quayle (ed.). *Mrs. Simcoe's Diary.* (Toronto: Macmillan of Canada, 1965).

Jameson, Anna Brownell. *Winter Studies and Summer Rambles in Canada.* (Toronto: McClelland and Stewart, 1990).

Keller, Helen. *The Story of My Life.* (New York: Delacorte Press, 1980).

Kilbourn, William. *The Firebrand: William Lyon Mackenzie and the Rebellion in Upper Canada.* (Toronto: Clarke, Irwin, 1956).

Kiwanis Club of Stratford, Ontario, Inc. *Niagara Falls, Canada: A History of the City and the World Famous Beauty Spot. An Anthology.* (Niagara Falls, ON: Kiwanis Club, 1967).

Kriner, T.W. *In the Mad Water: Two Centuries of Adventure and Lunacy at Niagara Falls.* (Buffalo, N.Y: J & J Publishing, 1999).

Leslie, W. Bruce. *Collapse of Falls View Bridge and Ice Jam of 1938.* (Niagara Falls, ON: F.H. Leslie, Ltd., 1938).

McGreevy, Patrick. *Imagining Niagara; The Meaning and Making of Niagara Falls.* (Amherst: University of Massachusetts Press, 1944).

Morden, James C. *Historic Niagara Falls.* (Niagara Falls, ON: The Lundy's Lane Historical Society, 1932).

Parkman, Francis. *LaSalle and the Discovery of the Great West.* (Toronto: New American Library of Canada, 1963).

Petrie, Francis. *Roll Out the Barrel: The Story of Niagara's Daredevils.* (Erin, ON: Boston Mills Press, 1985).

Seibel, George A. *Bridges Over the Niagara Gorge: Rainbow Bridge - 50 Years, 1941-1991.* (Niagara Falls, ON: Niagara Falls Bridge Commission, 1991).

_____. *The Niagara Portage Road: A History of the Portage on the West Bank of the Niagara River.* (Niagara Falls, ON: City of Niagara Falls, 1990).

_____. *Ontario's Niagara Parks – 100 Years. Centennial, 1885-1985.* (Niagara Falls, ON: Niagara Parks Commission, 1985).

Sharpiro, Dean. *Blondin.* (St. Catharines, ON: Vanwell Publishing, 1989).

Sowell, Mike. *July 2, 1903; The Mysterious Death of Hall-of-Famer Big Ed Delahanty.* (New York: Macmillan, 1992).

Stanley, George F.G. *The War of 1812. Land Operations.* (Macmillan of Canada in Collaboration with the National Museums of Canada, 1983).

T.C. *A Ride to Niagara in 1809.* (Rochester, N.Y: Reprinted from *The Portfolio* for July, August, September and October 1810, for George P. Humphrey, 1915).

Tiplin, A.H. *Our Romantic Niagara; A Geological History of the River and the Falls.* With Additional Material by George Seibel. (Niagara Falls, ON: Niagara Falls Heritage Foundation, 1988).

Whalen, Dwight. *The Lady Who Conquered Niagara: The Annie Edson Taylor Story.* (Brewer, Maine: Edson Genealogical Association, 1990).

Newspapers

Niagara Falls, Ontario, *Daily Record.* Various Issues.

Niagara Falls, New York, *Gazette.* Various Issues.

Niagara Falls, Ontario, *Review.* Various Issues.

Toronto, Ontario, *Globe* (Later *Globe and Mail*). Various Issues.

Photo by George Bailey.

About the Author

A retired teacher, Sherman Zavitz has had a fascination with the history of Niagara Falls and area for many years. He is a past president of The Lundy's Lane Historical Society and has served on the boards of the Canadian Canal Society, the Friends of Fort George and the Niagara Falls Museums.

He has been recognized for his historical expertise by being appointed Official Historian for both the City of Niagara Falls, Ontario and The Niagara Parks Commission.

The author of a number of books about Niagara Falls' heritage, he has also written a weekly newspaper column for the Niagara Falls *Review* since 1993. He is a frequent speaker on historical topics, conducts an annual walking tour and has been a step-on Niagara tour guide for over 25 years.